The Mighty Oak

Nature

•

Navy

•

Nation

By Michael Fass

First published in Great Britain in 2023
by Michael Fass, The Coach House, Old Gore, Ross on Wye,
Herefordshire,
HR9 7QT

Author's website
www.napoleon-on-st-helena.co.uk

Cover design by John Fass

Photographs design by Fay Dorrington

Printed by
Biddles Limited, King's Lynn
www.biddles.co.uk

ISBN 978-1-3999-4742-8

This book is dedicated to

my dear wife without whose constant support and encouragement this book has nevertheless been written

&

to my good friend,
Stephen Barran

Also by Michael Fass

'The Vital Economy' with Richard Scothorne (1990)

'Faith in Governance' with Michael Willis (2004)

'The Resilient Director' with Tony O'Rourke & Michael Willis (2005)

'Salute Me When You See Me' (2016)

'Napoleon's Drop' (2019)

'The Royal Berkshire Regiment – The Early Years' (2021)

'Napoleon@bay – Exile & Death' (2021)

Contents

NOTE: The dates shown in the text are Anno Domini or AD

Introduction

The mighty oak has played a significant part in England's – and later Britain's – cultural, economic and historic story and never more so than during the long war with revolutionary France. The oak tree has had a symbolic and practical role in many aspects of the nation's life and in the creation and development of what, until the seventeenth century, was known as the Navy Royal, defender of our liberties and described as the "wooden walls of England". This is its story.

The clue is in the name in at least two ways. First, I was brought up as a child at Oakley Green, a coaching green in East Berkshire on the post-chaise route between Reading and the town of Windsor with its great castle, whose battlements I could see on a fine day. Windsor has been home to the kings and queens of England since the time of Duke William of Normandy, the Conqueror.

Speaking of whom, William – it was believed by his hagiographers – had been conceived on the night that Heleve, his mother, the daughter of a tanner, had entered Falaise Castle in Normandy, having attracted the attention of Duke Robert of Normandy. Robert had espied her far below from a castle window whilst she was doing her washing in the town's public ablutions shed and was instantly attracted to her as she tucked up her skirt a little too high at her waist.

The story has it that on their first night together, after finally falling asleep, Heleve dreamt of an oak tree springing out between her legs with its branches spreading across Europe. This was to happen in the next hundred years when the various Norman kingdoms dominated the European continent and the near Middle East including those of Antioch, Cyprus, England, Greece, Jerusalem, Italy, Malta and Sicily.

An early genealogical tree shows Heleve's son William, now King of England, surmounted by two tall and twisting oak trees, decorated with lush leaves, acorns and wildlife (Royal MS 14B VI, British Library). The mighty oak has a long pedigree as a national image.

Second, my surname Fass, literally means *barrel* in German although I prefer to interpret the word as *cooper,* the man who makes oak barrels.

On the east side of Oakley Green flows the stately Thames, down which the East India Company's timber was floated from its depot at Reading into its dockyards at Deptford in London. On the west side, lies Windsor Forest, whose oak trees were planted by William over 800 years ago to provide him with the timber for the nation's navy.

On the road that runs along the edge of the Forest, there were four public houses: The Prince of Wales, the Braywood Inn, the Red Lion and the Nags Head, where passengers could slake their thirst on the dusty journey.

Almost opposite the Braywood Inn stood a gate into the Forest which we used to enter on our ponies or on foot. Under the great canopy of trees the world seemed to us children to be a sombre place and we spoke in whispers. Oak forests grow on sacred ground.

Behind The Prince of Wales public house stood an old smithy where the village blacksmith – the Vulcan of mythology – shoed our ponies every holidays whilst I worked his leather hand bellows.

I have become interested in oaks, timber, ships and shipbuilding as a consequence of my research and writing about the period of Napoleon's exile and death on St Helena (1815-1821).

The ex-emperor was taken down to the South Atlantic in HMS *Northumberland,* a third-rater (that is, a warship with three gun decks and 74 guns) after surrendering to the British off the coast of France in July 1815.

On St Helena, Napoleon was guarded on land by HM 66th Foot (Berkshire), whose First Battalion had arrived from India on the storeship *Dorah,* that had been in-country built in Bombay. At sea, Napoleon was guarded by the Royal Navy's Island Squadron whose captains included Fred Marryat, the author of *Children of the New Forest,* commanding HMS *Beaver.*

From my research, I have come to appreciate that it was the industrial infrastructure of Britain that played the major part in the defeat of revolutionary and Napoleonic France – and of its emperor.

The focus of the history in the period has traditionally been on Wellington's campaigns and the heroic deeds of those who slogged up and down the Iberian Peninsula suffering the dust, dirt and deprivations of six long years of hard fighting against a ruthless enemy. This is understandable given the number of first-hand accounts that exist, written by those who were present at the great battles of Albuera and Talavera and at the sieges of Badajoz and Cuidad Rodrigo, battles in which so much British blood and treasure was expended over so many years,

However, there is another story to be told which is about the truly monumental efforts that were made in Britain's shipyards and associated industrial enterprises and depots that more than equalled the efforts of Wellington's army – but without its romantic appeal.

Britain's industrial revolution had started earlier in the eighteenth century and by the time that war broke out in the 1790s, the country had already become the world's leading industrial power. The discovery and use of coal; the invention of steam driven machinery and the mastery of the production of iron, had all fuelled the nation's ability to fight on an industrial scale.

Nowhere could this be seen more clearly than in Britain's shipyards, both military and commercial. These yards formed the backbone of Britain's war effort alongside the gun shops of Birmingham; the cannon works in Falkirk; the military supply depot at Weedon Bec in Northamptonshire and the hundreds of smithies up and down the country whose smiths forged iron nails.

Emblematic of the role of industry in winning the war was the mechanisation of pulley block making in the Royal Navy's Portsmouth dockyard and the manufacture of ships nails at Chatham. Both of these products represented the standardisation of production which, whilst very familiar to the modern world, were innovations that at the time revolutionised output and without which victory would have been much delayed or impossible.

After graduation, I joined The Proprietors of Hays Wharf Ltd, a shipping, lighterage and wharfage company that boasted *300 years on London's river* located in the Upper Pool of the Thames opposite the Tower of London. Here, amongst 9,500 dock staff, I was trained as an organisation and methods analyst, responsible for the productivity of staff and the quayside warehouses in which they worked. Later in my career with Hays, I managed a production facility in Scotland, the largest of its kind in Europe, which produced 4.5 million cases of Scotch whisky for export each year. The Bond at Strathleven Warehouses in Dumbarton employed eighteen coopers who crafted and repaired over 8,000 fifty-six gallon hogsheads made of Canadian or Spanish oak.

As a result, ideas about innovation, mechanisation, productivity and the automation of industrial processes have never been far from my mind. I have renewed these interests here in telling the story of Britain's heroic efforts in the Napoleonic era.

Of all the materials that were vital to the Napoleonic war effort, the use of oak timber for all kinds of purposes was by far and away the most critical.

It takes over a hundred years to grow an oak tree; more than two thousand oak trees are used in the construction of a third-rater and one thousand wooden pulley blocks are needed for hauling the ship's sails up and down and running its cannon in and out of their ports.

Without the combination of natural product and advanced manufacturing, Britain could not have won the war. The French simply had nothing like it.

This book tells the story of the oak and its role in securing victory that included the stunning defeat over the French fleet at Trafalgar in 1805 and the final victory of Britain and her allies at Waterloo in 1815.

There are other connections between the oak tree, national culture and our history. Public houses called *The Royal Oak* are the most numerous in the country. These are named in honour of the oak tree that sheltered Charles II after his defeat at the second battle of Worcester in September 1651. After the battle, Charles fled into Shropshire pursued by Parliamentary troops and was obliged to hide in an oak tree for the night, later known as the *Boscobel* oak, named after the estate on which it stood. Charles subsequently escaped and took flight for France from Shoreham Quay in Sussex. When I worked for Hays, Shoreham was owned by the company and I spent time at the port.

The oak leaf became a symbol of defiance against Cromwell's republican rule and when the Stuart monarchy was restored in 1660, and Charles became King Charles II, Parliament voted that the 28th May, the date of his restoration, should be a national holiday and named it *Oak Apple Day.* The same day is marked as Founders Day at the Royal Hospital, Chelsea when the In-patients wear a sprig of oak on their scarlet tunics.

The oak leaf became a quasi-national emblem and is carried, for example, in the form of a wreath surmounting the colours of a regiment on the days when its battle honours are commemorated.

I have a sprig of oak branch on either side of my front door to remind visitors of the loyalties of the house. The oak tree signifies strength, character and stability and the tree is associated with the Nation's pride, health and history.

Finally, on the occasion of her late majesty, Queen Elisabeth II's funeral on the 19th September 2022, it was said that the wreath on her coffin included oak leaves signifying the strength of love.

The book is in three parts. The first part tells the story of the oak tree in England's cultural and natural history. The second part explains the role of the oak tree in the economy and, in particular, in the development of the Royal Navy and in the third part the way that this led to Great Britain's position as a global power.

A note of caution. The study of history inevitably reflects the idiosyncratic and co-incidental interests of those who undertake it. This book is an acute example of the genre on the journey that it takes through the forest.

Chapter One The Knower of the Oak Tree

The mighty oak has been at the foundation of England's cultural and natural story. Not only as a part of England's ancient landscape, but also involved in the mystery of the forest and its secrets, the oak tree has stood as a symbol for early religion and the worship of old gods.

At the end of the Second Ice Age (c.120,000BC) as the ice receded and the human population of Europe began to move northwards again, the land was covered, first, with bush and shrub and then with trees; oak, ash and pine. The whole land was a dense forest into which humans entered at their peril.

The forest was dark and forbidding. Strange noises could be heard within it: the sound of birds and animals moving amongst the trees and in the thickets, and, always the sigh of the wind; the rustle of the oak bough and the roar of the storm.

Little wonder that the ancients were frightened to enter the forest from the small settlements that they had carved out of it. Of course, they were obliged to enter the forest for reasons of economy. The forest provided a part of their diet; building materials for their homes; acorns for their flour; food for their pigs in autumn and charcoal for their fires. Most important of all, they had to enter the forest in order to clear more of it to make the space to create their fields.

None of these things made these early people *like* the forest; they entered it because they had to, that is, with the exception of one group of individuals: Their priests or *shamans.* We call them Druids, a Celtic word meaning priest, magician or soothsayer; a demiurge or the Knower of the Oak Tree. The Druids were responsible for worship and sacrifice, often believed to have included humans.

The Druids derived their power over the imagination by having no fear of the forest and embracing it as their source of knowledge and regeneration. They focussed on the sacred nature of the oak tree and the mysterious parasite that grows in its branches. Mistletoe represented the fecundity that the Druids also depicted in the Green Man of antiquity.

Whilst the Romans destroyed the political influence of the Druids, belief in their powers was never entirely eliminated, the evidence for which can be seen today in the blacked-up faces of Morris dancers as they perform their ritual dances. These are often accompanied by music and rhythmic steps that are similar to the trance-dances of other peoples and cultures throughout the world. The dancers blackened forms represented all that was dangerous about the ancient forest; its darkness and silence; its sense of isolation and unknowning-ness. In England, these dances are often observed on the First of May, or Mayday each year, when the ceremony of *Jack of the Green* is re-enacted and the children of the village dance around a maypole. In Fownhope, Herefordshire (a village close to where I now live), a procession is held by the *Heart of Oak Society* led by its master carrying a pole topped with oak leaves and followed by a brass band. Much drink is taken along their way!

The tradition of the medieval Mummers was also one that included elements of these ancient rituals that were often focused on the theme of death and re-birth performed around the time of the Christian celebration of Christmas whose timing was derived from the earlier Druidic period of the New Year with its promise of Spring.

The Green Man

However, the place where the tradition of the Green Man is most recorded is by its presence in churches up and down the land. In Rosslyn Chapel, Midlothian, there are, famously, ninety-three of them.

In many images and in many places, both secular and religious, *The Green Man*, also known as a *foliate head,* often half hidden in a wreath of oak leaves, can be seen peering out in a sinister half-human, half-animal form. The Green Man is often depicted as a thing of sorrow, perhaps representing the loss of the natural world of the forest, compared to the orderly world of the camp. The Green Man can conjure up sinister fantasies of the eerie and macabre as the sound of the silence of the forest preys on the mind and their lolling tongues and unruly moustaches do little to help the human mind from becoming full of foreboding.

It is in churches throughout England and Western Europe that the most images of the Green Man can be found on roof bosses, corbels, tombs, screens and pew ends and there is a good reason for their presence.

When St Augustine landed on the Saxon shore in 597 he found a great variety of folk religions flourishing amongst its pagan population. The Christians already practising their religion were far too few to insist that popular rites associated with the oak should be eliminated and so these rites were brought inside the church; their power was tamed and they became mere church decoration. They lost their potency as an image of worship to a greater power.

Today, the Green Man, and its close association with the oak tree, continues to fascinate. Whilst its power may have diminished in the modern mind, the *Knower of the Oak Tree* reminds us of the remote past and of our ancestors who lived in and around the ancient forests of our land. This image of the oak that is so quintessentially English.

Chapter Two *from Tiny Acorns……*

The mighty oak is the best known and best loved tree in the English landscape. Oak trees take 100 years to mature and last for generations. Oaks define the countryside throughout the land and are the home of the animals, birds and insects that are common to our natural world.

Natural & Human Origins

The most memorable tree in the forest is the oak tree. The oak tree's girth, height, age and conformity mark it out as highly significant and it has been a feature of natural history and human culture throughout the world for thousands of years.

Since the final retreat of the glaciers in the last Ice Age, the oak has been one way to define civilisation as its timbers have been used to build houses, wagons, ships, windows and barrels. Along its radii, planks can be split to any length or width and nowhere has this been more important than in the manufacture of ships, either dug out with primitive stone tools or clinker-built by ancient people. In the Viking age, one of the hey-days of early ship building, oaken long boats were buried with the dead along with other oak artefacts including coffins, treasure chests, vats and oak corks.

Across the whole of the temperate world, in Asia, Europe and North America, the oak tree grew alongside the earliest human settlements, but pre-dated them by many millions of years.

Of the many attributes of the oak tree, none was more important than the acorn, not only because it was the progenitor of the next generation of oak trees, but also because it provided the basis for the human diet. Acorns were the staple of early human settlement and known in many languages as *meal bearing* trees.

Whilst males were more likely to act as hunters, females acted as food gatherers and acorns formed the basis of a group's diet. Even today, in the Middle East, the sap of an oak tree is called *manna,* a juice that is mixed with egg, almond and spices to make a sweet cake. Acorn flour is still used to bake bread in Corsica, Sardinia and parts of North Africa and is prized for its keeping qualities. In

Spain, salted acorns are still enjoyed as snacks and acorn oil is used as an alternative to olive oil.

The Pliocene age had folded the land into steep ridges but the Pleistocene age that followed had scoured it with ice with only small areas of fertile land remaining. Here, oak trees survived until the ice had receded and oaks began to cover the fertile lands of the Middle East before spreading into the Mediterranean and as far North as Scandinavia ten thousand years ago.

It was in the folds of these ridges and in such temperate climates, that human beings emerged, hunting game, searching for crabs and mussels on the sea shore and harvesting wild grains before the domestication of animals, whilst relying on acorns as their staple.

Harvesting and storing acorns cost much less labour than wheat and barley and village communities could gather sufficient acorns in three weeks to last two or three years. Such bounteous harvests were known as oak *masts* and became the basis for the Medieval practice of *pannage,* the right of villagers to fatten pigs in the forest before they were slaughtered before Christmas.

For more than three thousand years, people lived on acorns supplemented by meat, grains, herbs and spices. Paradoxically, the settled nature of this way of life led to migration made possible by the bounty of the oak tree and its fruit. As the earth warmed and oak forests expanded, humans could travel northwards ending up in Northwest Europe and Scandinavia. The root of the word for oak is *dru,* from which the word *druid* is formed; the oak tree's earliest human adherents.

Hearts of Oak

As a key material in support of human life, the oak had no parallel and has been used by humans since the earliest of times. Oak was used not only for the small items of everyday life such as fencing, poles, stakes, beds, barrels and axles, but also for larger projects such as oak walks and-roadways, bridges, doors, houses, palisades, henges, coffins and boats. Chords of oak for firewood were a principal item of audit in Duke William's remarkable account of his possessions in the *Domesday Book* produced in 1086.

Oak made travel possible through bogs, swamps and fens. The first buildings and furniture were made of oak. The first boats were made of oak planks that had been split, sewn with willow and waterproofed with pitch. Whilst Britain's oak forests were both feared and respected by human inhabitants, they provided some of the most important materials for human life that included its timber, firewood, tanbark, charcoal, fence, hurdle poles and acorns.

However, by the end of the Middle Ages, the forests of England had been reduced to less that 15% of its total land mass and oak became scarce as farming and agriculture became a priority. Some husbandry of the remaining forest areas was practised, for example, at Windsor, in the Forest of Dean, the New Forest in Hampshire, in Savernake Forest in Wiltshire, in Sherwood in Nottinghamshire and in Sussex as the kings and queens of England recognised their importance for the defence of the realm. However, the pressure on oak forests was intense as the demands of shipbuilders and other uses for the material rose continually. All-in-all, the oak tree was the most versatile and productive of all the species in the forest.

The oak produced the fruit of the acorn that fed ancient people before the days of their settlement and the introduction of agriculture. The oak produced timber that could be cut, carved and shaped for human use in a wide variety of settings including barns, houses and boats. The oak's bark could be used for tanning and its galls – the tiny blemishes made by insects on its leaves – could be crushed to produce ink.

The oak tree – A natural multiplier

In addition to its uses by humans, the oak was the greatest multiplier in the forest and many tasks of nature were performed under its canopy. The oak has a root system that is more than ten times its girth above ground and has a long life of many hundreds of years when left undisturbed. The oak produces millions of acorns and is the home to countless creatures. Jays are particularly partial to acorns and collect them into their stores each autumn as well as distributing acorns far and wide across the landscape. Jays are the greatest help to the germination of oaks of all the creatures of the forest and a multiplier of their own.

Woodpeckers nest in the oak's holes and crevices and badgers, ducks, pheasants, mice, voles and, squirrels all feast on the acorn harvest. These in turn attract birds of prey such as owls, kestrels and sparrow hawks which nest in its branches. To meet these demands, every three or four years, oak trees produce *mast,* a harvest so plentiful that the creatures who rely on the acorn crop cannot consume it all leaving more acorns available for seeding new oaks.

Oak trees are also the home to every kind of insect that make their home on its leaves and in its acorns. Weevils burrow into the acorn and live off its sweet centre until they are hatched or are caught earlier by other predators, for example, ants, who find safety inside the acorn. Almost a third of all acorns are destroyed in this way long before they fall to the ground and germinate. It has also been said that *the bramble is the nursery of the oak.*

Caterpillars, insects and moths live in oak trees which is one reason for the numbers of birds that visit oak trees. In addition to the multitude of moths, butterflies, gall wasps, mammals and birds that use an oak tree for food and shelter, there are also many species who live at the foot of the oak and use its leaf litter and mould. These include earthworms and mushrooms. Even when oaks grow old, lose their inner trunk, and become hollowed out, they create a large space in which bats and birds can nest, particularly owls.

The mighty oak that dominates the landscape; the dependable oak that harbours creatures; the durable oak that keeps its secrets; the wise oak that admonishes and commends; the fertile oak that feeds and equips; the noble oak that defends the nation: The oak tree is simply the most precious and productive tree in the forest and of human history.

Chapter Three: ......Mighty Oak Trees Grow

In past times the mighty oak provided the materials for the daily lives of Britons including the timber for their halls and houses, the planking for their ships, the bark for their leather clothing, the shoes for their feet , the harness for their horses and even the gall for their ink. The oak tree's trunk and branches were the most sought after of all the trees in the forest and its cultivation provided employment not only for the woodcutters and master shipwrights of the royal dockyards and their staff but also the colliers who manufactured charcoal and the barkers and tanners who processed leather.

Wood cutters had been entering the forest since the earliest of times to fulfil the needs of their community for building materials. At first, using primitive tools made from wood and stone, wood cutters had laboured to fell suitable trees for their use and the oak was one of the most prized trees of the forest.

It grew straight and tall. It was strong and hard but could be worked along its seams into planking and was adaptable for many uses. From the earliest times, oak trees were used for ship and boat building and so prized were they that the oak tree became a part of the royal prerogative with kings and princes exercising their power to establish growing and cutting rights throughout their domains.

Royal forests were created with the specific aim of providing oak timber for the monarch's ship building programme and restrictions were placed on private forests or *parks* in which oak trees were planted, grew and were harvested. These so-called parks had their origin in the Middle Ages when the open spaces of the forest were impaled, that is, fenced, to contain the herds of deer which were kept for the king's pleasure.

The demands on the harvesting of oak were tremendous as houses and whole towns and cities were built of oak timber and there were times when there was simply insufficient oak to go round. Oak plantations were highly prized and both restrictions on cutting oak trees down and incentives for its planting and care were passed by Parliament and demanded by rulers. No requirement was so urgent as the need for the building of warships in the royal dockyards as first England and later Britain, developed its sea power. The royal dockyards had an insatiable demand for oak timber. It took many years for an oak to grow before it could be used by the shipwrights. Up to two thousand oaks or the same number of loads – one load being approximately one ton – taken from sixty acres of forest, were required to supply the needs for the construction of a single Third rater.

The naval shipwrights in the royal dockyards at Chatham and Portsmouth , and their civilian counterparts at Deptford, sent search parties into the great forests of England in pursuit of oak trees and Chatham's shipwrights travelled throughout the length and breadth of the country searching for the right trees.

Contractors extended the Navy's search for suitable trees and oaks were felled in Bedfordshire, Norfolk, Suffolk, Surrey, Sussex and in Sherwood and Waltham forests and many other woodland areas. In addition, iron shot came from the Renishaw estate in Derbyshire; guns were manufactured in the Weald of Kent and Sussex and gunpowder was made at mills in the Lea valley in Essex.

The search parties were often led by naval officers on shore duty and, in one famous example, a party led by Admiral Sir Horatio Nelson, lodged in Ross on Wye while searching the nearby Forest of Dean for oak.

The woodcutters left their mark on the landscape as they progressed through the forest. Cutting down mature oak trees was a hard task and oak made a very heavy load for the teams of horses that were required to haul it out of the forest. Forest tracks were poor and only major roads could be used for transport. Often, rivers were a vital means of conveyance for the timber to be floated down waterways and canals and into timber yards or ports. Overland journeys took time and added to expense; the biggest timbers could take up to two years to reach the dockyard. The East India Company's yard in Reading was the largest of its kind in Britain supplying both its own needs at Deptford and selling timber to the royal dockyards on the Thames, in the Medway and at Portsmouth.

Surveyors sent from the dockyard inspected the trees in the forest and selected the timber for cutting. The ideal timber came from an oak tree of at least one hundred years old that would be sufficiently mature to yield *compass* oak that would be ideal for the many shapes and sizes needed in ship building. Compass oak was an oak tree whose branches grew out to a 360° radius that were naturally curved and bent that could be used in various parts of the ship's construction, including bends, floors, futtocks, keels, knees, ribs, scarfs, sternposts and transoms. Each of these were the most prized parts of the compass oak's naturally growing branches and commanded high prices.

When the timber arrived in the dockyard, it was stacked in the open air for up to two years whilst it dried out before being used in ship construction.

Imagination was needed to recognise the value of the compass timber that was so sought after by the shipwrights. Whether it was a First rater with 120 guns on four decks or a sloop with a crew of twelve, all of the Navy's ships were made from 90% oak. Oak was the material of choice for its toughness; strength, water resistance and cleavability as well as its long branches at right angles to its trunk. The woodcutters looked for two features in particular: Large, bent or crotched pieces from which the frame of the ship could be built and long straight timber that could be sawn into planking for sides and floors.

The surveyors also took account of the land in which the oak trees stood. Thin soils often meant the presence of windblown trees that might have come down because of some defect in their roots whilst the largest trees were beyond their prime. Trees growing in deeper soil and closer to water would remain much sounder for longer.

When the tree was cut, the surveyor tapped its trunk listening for hollowness before ordering the woodcutters to lop off the branch wood and make a saw pit for cutting the larger straight lengths into ship's planking. Templates were placed over the key compass parts in situ so that the shapes could be cut as accurately as possible; carrying out the preliminary work of the dockyard. Even after all the hard labour used to fell and prepare the product of the tree for transportation, the surveyor could still be sorely disappointed as boles, knots and twists could all spoil its quality and make it worthless for the dockyard except for firewood.

In addition, shipbuilding did not represent the only challenge of supply and oak was sought after for many other purposes.

Colliers & Charcoal

A major use of oak was the production of charcoal which was used by local ironworkers and blacksmiths. Charcoal was used to intensify the heat of the forge and – helped further by the use of bellows- raised the temperature of the fire that enabled blacksmiths to produce a wide variety of vital artefacts including swords, bells, cannon, coinage, hinges, nails, ploughs and pots. Colliers were considered to be part of forest lore and lived in primitive conditions throughout the summer season. The collier used chords of oak to form a conical pile up to twelve feet high with a chimney at its centre. The pile was then covered in soil before it was lit by dropping burning coals down its chimney. A slow burn without the wood bursting into flame was critical and the collier looked after between ten and twenty piles at a time for twenty four hours a day that burned for between two and fifteen days depending on size and weather conditions.

Barkers & Tanning

Another important use of the oak tree was in the production of tannin for the leather trades. It is no accident that tanneries were set up on the edge of town to carry out their trade. It was filthy and stinking work as the hides of newly slaughtered animals arrived at the tannery. The tanners work was dirty and heavy as the raw hides had to be cleaned up as their hoofs, hair, fat and gore were removed before they were pounded, washed, scrubbed and stretched.

The tanners work absolutely stank and the location of the tannery was highly regulated to make sure they were not situated up-wind or up-stream of other dwellings. Worst of all, part of the preparation for the tanning process, was to soak the hides in a solution of fermented chicken dung.

However, until the invention of artificial, man-made materials, leather was the basis for the needs of everyday life and artefacts that included: shoes, sandals and boots, bottles, harnesses and straps for machinery.

The barkers, often working in family groups, followed the tree cutters into the forest and, after the oak had been felled, cut rings around its trunk before removing the bark. When the bark had been ground down to a powder, it was soaked in water with the hides and released tannins that prevented the skin from rotting and made it supple and almost waterproof.

The actual tanning process was ancient and complex. The hides were softened in vats of water before being removed and scraped over a log to remove any remaining fat or hair before the hide was placed in the tanning vat for anything up to a year as the hide matured into leather. The hide was then placed on a table where the currier rubbed oil and dyes onto its surface to make the leather subtle and suitably coloured.

From tiny acorns……Mighty oak trees grow

All-in-all, the oak tree was the most versatile and productive of all the species of the forest. The oak produced the fruit of the acorn that fed ancient people before the days of their settlement and the introduction of agriculture. The oak produced timber that could be cut, carved and shaped for human use in a wide variety of settings including barns, houses and boats. The oak's bark could be used for tanning and its galls – the tiny blemishes made by insects on its leaves – could be crushed to produce ink.

Chapter Four — Frames & Futtocks

Frame, futtock and scarf were words that were most familiar to the shipwrights and their contractors who roamed the forests in search of good compass oak from which the parts of a ship would be cut and shaped. Ship construction was a complex undertaking that required skills developed over hundreds of years by generations of experts. By the mid-eighteenth century, the royal dockyards had become the Nation's greatest industrial enterprise not only employing thousands to build the ships but also all of its accessories including masts, cannon, sails and supplies.

The Shipwrights Arms

Of all the men in the dockyard, the shipwrights were the foremost of the trades. Shipwrights were in charge of the construction of any ship, from the laying of the keel to the fitting of the upper decks. Shipwrights were also responsible for the repair of ships in dry dock and removing and replacing the ship's rotten timbers, sometimes down to their keel.

The sound of the axe in the forest was one of the oldest in civilisation. Ancient people built their canoes from hollowed-out trees either using primitive axes or by burning out the trunk leaving a hard shell. The first oak-built vessels were constructed over c.4,000 years ago made from oak planks that were stitched together with yew withies or supple branches which were then caulked or waterproofed, with moss and thin oak laths, or strips.

These early craft used paddle-power to drive them through the water until sails were introduced. These craft were propelled by oarsmen with up to fifty on either side. Later, warships with strong pointed bows were designed to spear the enemy. The alternative to these craft were the rafts of Egypt and the oceans of the Pacific which were made from bundles of reeds tied together.

Later, ships were constructed either by the *carvel* method, that is with the sides made of planking edge to edge, or by the *clinker* method, that is with the timbers overlapping each other. Viking ships, for example, were clinker built.

In the Middle Ages the predominant design in use was the *Cog,* a clinker built vessel that was made famous by the sailors of the Hanseatic League whose maritime headquarters were at Lubeck on the Baltic coast.

From here, a network of coastal nations, ports and warehouses dominated the trade of Northern Europe. Cologne, Danzig, Hamburg and Lubeck were the League's largest outposts, but Hull, Kings Lynn and London each had their *steelyards* where the Hanseatic merchants were permitted to stay and conduct their business. In London, the Hanse merchants anchored their cogs in the Upper Pool, opposite the Tower of London. Many of their vessels could carry up to 50 Tuns (equivalent to 240 gallons) of much sought after herring in barrels.

Both ship construction methods required an internal frame onto which the planking was attached with nails made of wood, called *trenails,* which were round, tough wooden pins made of oak – and later iron – of various shapes and sizes, also known as dowels, which were driven into the planking and swelled in contact with water.

King Henry VIII brought shipwrights from Venice and Genoa to England to share their secrets with his master shipwrights. The oared galleys of Spain were useless in Atlantic waters and the king wanted vessels that could carry guns. The new ships that were wider and deeper in draught became the foundation of England's ship design as the shipwrights' art was passed from father to son. From 1500-1700, shipwrights and their teams built ships by eye, flair and rule of thumb and master shipwrights became the senior technical officers of the dockyard.

However, this began to change as scientific knowledge spread and by the end of the seventeenth century, mathematics, geometry and trigonometry were used in the calculations for the parts of the ship that would be cut and shaped to produce the rising and narrowing lines of the ship's hull shape. The master shipwright, in addition to being the key individual in the dockyard, was also an individual of respected for his wider knowledge. In 1711, William Sutherland, master shipwright and mariner, wrote an essay about his art beginning with the landowner who grew the oak trees and then described the best way to deal with timber for frames, planks and masts. In his essay, *The Shipbuilder's Assistant,* Sutherland referred to the latest ideas in mathematics, natural history and philosophy – or the shipwright's mysterious lines – including the study of the forms of fish and birds as a way to optimise the best shape for a ship. From these ideas came the optimum place on board for the ship's masts and ways to load and trim it.

The master shipwright was responsible for every aspect of the design of a new ship. Every dockyard had a *mould loft* where the shapes of all the parts of the ship were first drawn out to a scale of 1/48 on paper, before the shapes were cut to their actual size using thin wood or light battens on the mould loft floor. These would then be taken to the timber yard where they would be matched by the shipwrights' assistants as nearly as possible to the stock of timber and of the compass oak lying in its store.

In addition to their responsibility for the design and construction of new ships, the shipwrights were also responsible for the grounding, graving, docking and fitting out of the wet and dry docks of the yard and for the survey, repair, refit or scrapping of all the Navy's ships. These activities often outweighed the time spent on new construction.

The master shipwrights were also responsible for the employment of the dockyard's staff and maintenance of its buildings in addition to its stores and machinery.

The art of the shipwright was recognised in 1572 when the first master of the Shipwrights Company was appointed by King James I in 1605. A hundred years later, by the time of the reign of Queen Anne, England owned and managed one third of the total naval power of Europe

Frames & Futtocks

Frames, futtocks and scarfs were the joints that were fundamental to ship construction. Oak timbers in the yard were only between 6ft-12ft in length whereas the planking for the bottom, middle and top futtocks – the curved, tulip-shaped bends that formed the frame for the sides of the ship – needed to be much longer. These were joined together by scarf joints carved where the plank ends met before being pinned together with trenails or bolts. Cross beams were then secured using hanging knees fixed below the deck beams to join the structure together to make the ship's frame.

When the planking of the frame was completed, its seams were filled with *oakum,* which was made with loose, old rope mixed with pitch and tar before being pressed into the cracks by the caulkers using a mallet and caulking iron, a flat, blunt edged chisel. The caulkers were also responsible for the graving of ships either in dock or whilst lying on their sides. To *grave* meant to smear the ship's sides and bottom with a mixture of tallow from candles and tar, pitch and resin from fir trees to keep the hull watertight.

By 1759 out of 182 line of battle warships, 90 out of the total, or almost 50%, were Third raters with 74 guns. This was the standard, heavy battle ship of the Royal Navy that fought at Trafalgar with gun decks of 166 ft; keels of 136ft and breadths of 47ft. A completed Third rater weighed 1610 tons and consumed 2780 loads of oak timber or almost half of its felled weight. By this time, the royal dockyards were running out of English oak and relied on loads from the Adriatic, the Baltics and Canada in addition to larch, fir, mahogany, pine and teak from overseas plantations. As a way to protect hulls, lead sheathing was used instead of graving and, after 1761, sheets of copper were used to prevent fouling.

In 1805, at Trafalgar, of the thirty one ships engaged, seven were First raters of between 98 and 120 guns aged twenty years or more, whereas seventeen were Third raters of 74 guns and only thirteen years old. Both *HMS Victory* and *HMS Britannia* were over forty years old.

In addition to the use of axes, adzes, augers, hatchets and hammers, the shipwrights' staff used cross-cut saws in saw pits to cut the planking. In 1781, a 1370 tons ship, *HMS Agamemnon,* was built at Bucklers Hard on the Beaulieu River in Hampshire. She needed 2000 loads of timber (1 load = 1 ton) and took eighteen months to complete. She carried 64 guns and had a crew of 500.

By this time, suitable timber was growing very short as the Navy's needs grew from 320,000 tons of shipping in 1760 to 700,000 tons by 1805 with more than 900 vessels afloat. Shipwrights often took their moulds into the forest where they worked them up into shape to reduce waste and transport costs. Later, iron was used to make knees – the angled part that was used to join the beams to the sides of the ship – that were cheaper and stronger.

Masts, Sails & Stores

Ship's masts were stored in the dockyard either in mast lofts (dry) or mast ponds (wet). A ship of the line carried three masts, the largest of which, the main mast, that was placed in the middle of the ship. The foremast mast was positioned close to the bow and the mizzen mast between the main mast and the stern.

The masts were made in two or three interlocking sections which were joined together and stepped in the keelson (bottom of the ship) before passing through its lower decks before rising up to eighty feet above the main deck. Chatham's mast house lay beneath the mould loft where the timbers for the masts were turned and shaped. When ready for fitting into a ship, a special craft, usually a ship out of commission, came alongside to lift the mast into position using an on-board crane.

Ships had two kinds of rigging, or rope. Standing rigging, or stays, kept the masts upright and running rigging worked the sheets, or sails. In addition, ships needed rigging for anchor cables and mooring lines. At Chatham, the Navy's rope making facility was amongst its most important resources and employed over three hundred men. A 74 rater used c.20 miles of rigging and a typical warship in 1793, *HMS Valiant,* had 21 sails of various sizes that had been made in the dockyard's sail loft. Over 1000 pulley blocks were required to work them.

Cannons & Ordinance

Neither the ship's frame, sails and rigging, its sheets or its futtocks were the main purpose of the ship. The ship's main purpose was to act as a platform for its guns which were located in its sides. Ships were rated one, two or three, depending on the number of gun decks they carried and the standard was a three decker with 94 guns or Third rater.

The Ordinance Board was responsible for the supply of guns to the Navy as it was to the army. The Board designed guns and tested them before contracting their production to private suppliers, the most notable of which was the Carron Iron Works in Falkirk, Scotland.

The gun barrels were made using a mould of clay into which molten metal was poured. The gun was solid and had to be bored out using a drilling machine. The near end of the gun or *cascable,* with its rounded end button was added afterwards and reinforcing bands were added along the barrel's length.

Guns were rated by the weight of shot that could be discharged from them and the standard guns were either 32 or 42 pounders. In addition to the guns, ships were equipped with *carronades* or mortars which were placed on their quarterdecks, forecastles and poops and could fire up to 68 pounders at short distances. All the guns either below or on the main deck were placed in position on gun carriages that were run out for firing using block and tackle on either side which prevented the gun from rolling back from the shot's recoil. The gun could be elevated using a triangle of wood at the muzzle end. In bad weather, the guns were protected by gun ports that could be closed.

Gunpowder was manufactured in the mills at Waltham Abbey where a mixture of charcoal, saltpetre and sulphur was milled and mixed before the powder was poured into wooden casks. Once on board ship, the powder was kept in the ship's magazine under strictly controlled conditions. In addition to its main armament, ships carried a variety of small arms that were manufactured at the two royal small arms factories in the Lea Valley. These were issued from the ship's magazines to its detachment of Royal Marines before battle when action stations was sounded.

Ships in Ordinary

The great majority of the Navy's warships were kept in reserve or in *Ordinary* anchored offshore of the dockyard. Oak will not rot when it is either always wet or always dry. However, ships were neither and always exposed to the wind and weather whether afloat or ashore. This meant that ships were in a permanent state of decay whether they were in use or not. When afloat, but not in use, ships were the responsibility of a master carpenter and a skeleton crew of boatswain, carpenter, purser, cook and gunner who were responsible for carrying out maintenance and general repairs. Hatches and ports were opened or closed every day depending on weather conditions and the ship was kept aired. In good weather the ship's sides were watered morning and evening. Otherwise, she was an empty shell without guns, stores or main masts.

A ship going into ordinary was first inspected by a shipwright and surveyor before a warrant was issued specifying the repairs to be carried out before being handed over to the ship's boatswain who would then take responsibility for its upkeep.

Each year ships in ordinary were taken into the dockyard for caulking and painting. Sufficient ballast was loaded to keep the ship's bow and stern in the water to prevent too much drying out and sails were taken out and aired, surveyed and mended where needed.

Once a week the master shipwright of the dockyard sailed out and inspected the ship for any faults to ensure that the warrant for its maintenance was being followed.

Repairs & Refits

In addition to constructing new ships, which could only be done when King and Parliament made the funds available, the principal activity of the dockyard was the repair and refitting of ships already afloat. Hot summers and icy winters wrought havoc with the ship's timbers as fasteners became loose and timbers rotted.

The greatest concern was the hull which was permanently under water and became fouled by all manner of creatures that slowed the ship and made her almost impossible to steer. Ships were caulked inside and tallowed on the outside but such remedies did not last long. Hulls were sheathed in lead but this was not always effective as the lead reacted with the iron bolts used in some parts of the hull and joints became exposed as a result.

From 1778 onwards copper sheathing was introduced that kept ships' bottoms free from weeds which enabled them to sail faster and lessened the need for time in dock. Copper sheathing also provided protection from the *teredo* worm that destroyed the ship's hull in the tropics and had now spread into home waters.

Put into dry dock, and before sheathing was introduced, ships had weeds and barnacles burned and scrapped off and, after a long time at sea, new masts and new standing yards, rigging and sails were fitted.

The shipwrights had to gain access to the bowels of the ship when the structure of the ship had been damaged which could happen after battles at sea or in violent storms. On occasion, ships had to be stripped down to their hulls and completely rebuilt often using the timbers from a ship that had become beyond repair. The dockyard's work was relentless and as the Napoleonic wars approached, the shipwrights were obliged to meet the demands of an expanding Navy

HMS Victory

A British First rater of the eighteenth century mounting between 100-120 guns was a great floating fortress; a blunt instrument and the ultimate weapon of war. For a long time, Britain's naval architects and their royal masters had favoured fire power over manoeuvrability. *HMS Victory* was the ultimate testimony to this, with her 100 cannon and carronades lodged over three decks and able to fire over 1,100 lbs worth of broadside shot to her nearest rivals 812 lbs. She was enormous but what she lost in manoeuvre, she made up in fire power.

The ship was ordered to be built in 1758, one of only ten of her size in the whole of the century and construction started in 1759. After a 1/48th scale plan had been produced, full sized drawings were made on the floor of the mould loft before her keel was laid down. Seven scarfed keels were laid down one on top of another to form a keel that was of 150 feet in length. This was followed by the fitting of the stern post which was made of a single piece of oak after which the futtocks and frames were raised and the planking and decks were installed. When this part of her construction had been completed, she was stood in the yard for over three years for her timbers to season.

By now England's dockyards were desperately short of good timber and, whilst other parts of the ship, for example, her decks, could be made of fir, the main structure still demanded the finest quality oak. Rarest of all was compass timber that included branches that had two long arms growing at right angles that could be used as knees. *HMS Victory* would be a massive vessel and would require over 4,000 oak trees of all shapes and sizes.

Competition for oak timber was intense as England's landowners considered alternative offers from the private shipyards that were building the great merchantmen of the East India Company at the same time. Because of these shortages, work was stopped until

1763 when the ship's planking was completed and fittings were installed that included the anchor, masts, sails and rigging. After which the ship was painted. Traditionally, warships were painted red internally supposedly to disguise the blood stains that would be the consequence of battle. Finally, the ship was finished and *HMS Victory* was launched on the 7th May 1765.

However, whilst Britain had become the world's premier maritime power at the end of the Seven Years War, during which the public purse had been deep and the Royal Navy had stood at its highest in public esteem, *HMS Victory* held no commission on completion and served in a number lesser roles. First, she was placed in ordinary and rode at anchor with a skeleton crew in the Medway alongside many other vessels that were not required in peacetime. In 1797 she was anchored off Gillingham and used, first as a hospital ship and then to house French prisoners. However. In 1800 she re-entered Chatham dockyard and was prepared for war in which she would earn enduring glory.

Chapter Five   Barrels, Blocks and Nails

Of all the timber parts that went into a warship, none were more essential than the ships' pulley blocks that moved its sails up and down and helped to perform other vital tasks on board, for example hauling the ship's guns in and out of their ports. Pulleys were hand carved by craftsmen using hammer and chisel until a French engineer named Marc Brunel invented machinery that would manufacture blocks using a series of metal machines. The Block Mill at Portsmouth became the World's first in-line, automated production line.

The British national effort to defeat the continental armies throughout the nineteen long years of the Napoleonic wars was prodigious and only made possible by the earlier industrial revolution of the eighteenth century. Coal, steam, railways, canals and the industrialisation of many of the processes of production all made their contribution and these resources were harnessed by a government that employed many talented individuals in both military and civil positions of influence and authority.

With regards to the Royal Navy's contribution to the war effort and in addition to the work of the royal dockyards, many naval vessels were built in private yards on the Thames at Deptford and Rotherhithe by sub-contractors overseen by the Royal Navy's senior shipwrights.

Of course, a finished ship ready for sea was in itself very fine but it still needed to be supplied with its crew and stores of many kinds. For this purpose, the Royal Navy developed a series of subsidiary boards of management some under its direct control and others managed separately which led to all kinds of difficulties of co-ordination and lack of it.

The Ordinance Board provided guns for both the army and navy. and a Victualling Board provided all manner of consumables. A Transport Board chartered merchant ships to provide supplies to overseas garrisons and ships at sea. The Victualling Board managed depots, often provided by private contractors, throughout the country, and at ports including Hull, Newcastle, Leith, Whitehaven in Cumberland, Cork in Ireland and Falmouth in the South West. The Government also opened its own military warehousing complex at Weedon Bec in Northamptonshire.

Britain's canal network reduced the cost of freight dramatically and increased productivity compared to the meandering river systems of France. Livestock could be moved easily from rural areas to the victualling yards for fattening with over 40,000 beasts being reared in and around London each year.

Cattle and sheep were moved in great migrations across the whole of the British Isles by farmers, drovers and graziers in networks that stretched from the Scottish Highlands in the far north to Anglesey in the west, where cattle swam across the Menai Straights. The cattle making such journeys had to be shoed for their long journey by blacksmiths along their route. 20,000 bullocks were fattened on arrival each year in Norfolk and HM Ships were allocated live cattle on board. By 1813, 240,000 sheep were grazing on the Downs of southern England

When at sea the Fleet required continual replenishment and was supplied by convoys of storeships contracted by the Victualling Board and escorted by naval vessels. A warship carried 60 tons of coal for cooking on board and ships required great quantities of water in casks. The tonnage of water exceeded all the other provisions together and the 850 sailors of a 74 rater consumed three tons a day from 66 gallon hogsheads stored below decks.

The administrative arrangements required for the war effort were prodigious and would change the face of Britain forever. Nowhere was this more apparent than in the Royal Navy and its dockyards. Chatham alone employed hundreds of artisans and skilled workmen and the lesser dockyards and ports likewise. The whole nation entered into wartime working across both rural and urban areas and the bounds of business were expanded to cope. Sinecure in public office could no longer be tolerated and by the end of the war competent officials and managers had been introduced in both the public and private sectors of whom Sir Evan Nepean (1752-1822) served successively as Undersecretary at the Home Office, War Department and Admiralty.

Barrels

In addition to all the many other uses of oak, the manufacture of oak barrels was a major industry as well as being a vital material resource for the Royal Navy. Barrels were the main means of storage, preservation and transportation in ships throughout the world and the ship's cooper was a key non-commissioned officer on board Britain's warships. Barrels were durable, leak-proof, came in many sizes (Tuns, hogsheads, barrels, kilderkins, firkins and pins) and had many uses in daily life. These included the storage and transportation of water, wine, beer and cider, milk, butter and cheese, pickled and salted meats, fish and the vital vegetables that would prevent scurvy on long voyages.

A cooper's apprentice served his trade for seven years before being fully qualified in an ancient ceremony that included him being tarred and feathered before being rolled in a barrel by his peers. Often coopers and shipwrights worked side by side using inter-changeable skills.

Barrels were *dressed* using many of the same tools as shipwrights. First, the barrel staves were cut and shaped to produce a convex form. Next the staves of the barrel was *raised* and assembled. This was followed by the construction of the barrel ends before the barrel was bounded with iron hoops and bung holes cut into its top and end. Many cooperages were situated on the river's edge and close to a neighbouring shipyard. The transport trades depended on a steady supply of barrels and ships required many hundreds of them for every voyage to hold a wide variety of goods.

On board the Royal Navy's ships, the purser was a key officer. Pursers had to buy their commissions like any other officer of the wardroom, but also had to provide a bond to the Admiralty to secure their post and ensure their honesty. Pursers were often suspected by crews of short rationing and the embezzlement of funds to enrich themselves at the crew's expense but many were fastidious in their duties. Pursers were responsible for all consumables from candles and carrots to beef, butter and cheese. The purser had a wastage allowance of $1/8^{th}$ of the stores and could make money for himself by re-selling supplies either to the sailors or back to the government. He was also responsible for the purchase of small *necessaries* such as coal and wooden bowls which he had to pay for himself and await repayment which often took months or even years.

Oak barrels were the pallets of their day and were essential for the movement and storage of most goods in and out of warehouses, storerooms and cellars. Coopers worked in every community and were highly esteemed as indentured craftsmen. The Royal Navy had its fair share of uses for barrels both ashore and at sea where their contents were essential to the ship's mission.

Blocks

Over 1000 pulley blocks were required for a 74 rater warship. The use of blocks reduced the amount of energy required to move the weight, for example, of the ship's sails, to work its sheets (ropes); to move the guns in and out of its gun-ports; to raise masts; to work cranes, to lower the ship's boats and for many other tasks in the dockyard and on ships at sea.

Blocks were traditionally made with hammer and chisel by the dockyard carpenters and their manufacture was an absolute bottleneck in the launching of warships. The Royal Navy needed 100,000 blocks each year.

The war had encouraged manufacturing innovation and, in 1799, a French engineer named of Marc Brunel, the father of the ubiquitous Isambad, came to Britain as a refugee of the Revolution. Brunel peré had fled from France and first emigrated to America but had failed to raise sufficient interest in his ideas.

On his arrival in Britain Brunel, had made a fortuitous marriage to the sister of a chief clerk in the Navy Office and presented the clerk with drawings that showed the way that the manufacture of blocks could be mechanised utilising a number of machines.

The Royal Navy needed c. 100,000 blocks a year and it took 110 skilled labourers to make the quantity required. The method was expensive; the finished block's quality was variable and production was very slow.

The key to Brunel's invention was that his machines would be built of rigid iron frames set into the floor which would reduce vibration and the distortion of the wooden material of the block. Brunel's ideas were taken up by the Royal Navy and a production line was set up at Portsmouth.

Nails

Another innovation at Chatham was the standardisation of the production of nail making and supply at the dockyard. Nails for ships under construction required thousands of iron and wood nails of many shapes and sizes, known as *trenails.* These had always been made by contractors located in the many smithies in the counties of Kent and Sussex.

Smiths performed many forging tasks, for example, as chainsmiths, nailsmiths or oddsmiths, the latter making all kinds of forged items for the household including catches, latches, hinges and pins. Often these activities took place at home or in sheds attached to the dwelling where women and children worked long hours making small forged items. In the Black Country and around Dudley, Stourbridge and Wolverhampton such small forges abounded and the area became famous for its manufacturing activities.

The smithy was a busy place with local people bringing their broken hand tools, forks, hoes and spades and farmers their broken harrows and wheels. In addition ,the smith was also the local farrier and shoed the community's horses, oxen and ponies also acting as the local horse doctor and providing primitive cures for horses as well as other animals.

Working horses needed re-shoeing every three weeks and smiths kept a set of each animal's shoes for regular customers to save time spent in the smithy. The smith also kept stocks of other useful items including bolts, chains, gate furnishings and stable fittings which he purchased from travelling salesmen. The smith also looked after the cobs, hacks and hunters kept by the farmers and landowners. .

The forge was heated with charcoal, coal or coke and the smith's apprentice worked the leather bellows to maintain the temperature required. The most important item of equipment in the smithy was the anvil standing beside a trough of water to quench the forgings and to reduce the heat of the tools.

Smithies had been associated with the manufacture of ironwork since Roman times when the Kent coalfield had supplied coal and the southern counties had significant woodlands where the charcoal needed to heat the smithy's furnace was produced. However, in such a craft based industry it was inevitable that the quality of work of the many village smiths was variable and there were high wastage rates. As an alternative it was proposed by the shipwrights that the dockyard should produce a standard nail that could act as the pattern for the production of nails of every size and type.

After the examples had been prepared, the county blacksmiths were sent a single standard nail in a bag which they were instructed to forge and fill with fifty exact replicas of the model nail. They would be paid on the basis of the number of usable nails that they produced, rather than their weight.

As a result of these changes, standards in the dockyard were raised, production was increased and the wastage rate was reduced. It was the first example in the western world of the use of a standard unit of production in an industrial setting.

The story of the making of barrels, blocks and nails represented the extraordinary range and variety of artefacts produced by industry that contributed to final victory. Whilst barrels continue to be made using traditional methods, innovations such as block and nail making epitomised the inventiveness of Britain's naval industry; the supply of standardised goods and the ingenuity of commerce.

Much of the history of the Napoleonic wars has focussed on the long years of fighting on the Spanish Peninsular by an army that its leader, Lord Wellington, once described as ruffians and had remarked: "They may not frighten the enemy, but by God, they frighten me!" The same type of man working in the docks, machine shops and smithies of Britain also deserve a place alongside the heroes of the battles of Albuera and Talavera.

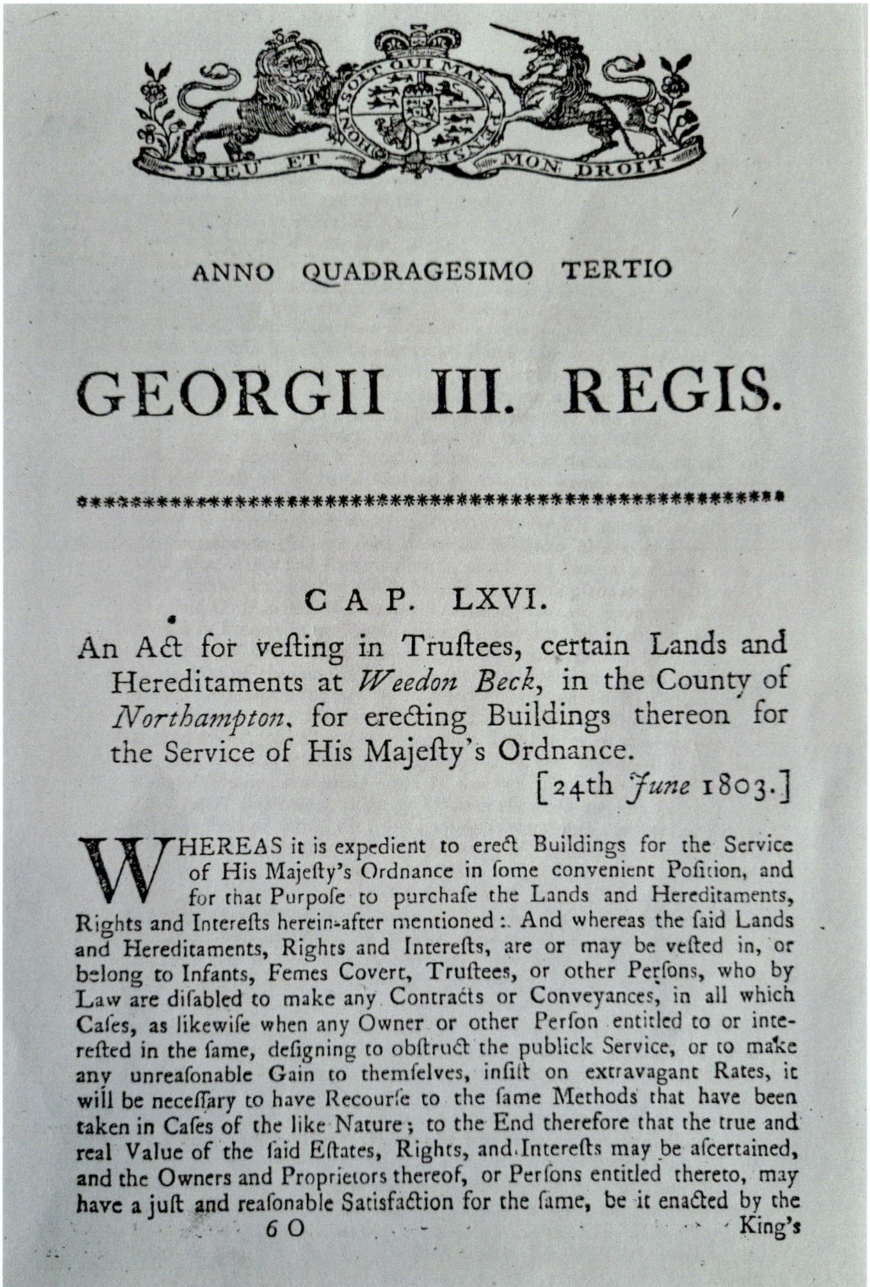

HONI SOIT QUI MAL Y PENSE

DIEU ET MON DROIT

ANNO QUADRAGESIMO TERTIO

GEORGII III. REGIS.

****

CAP. LXVI.

An Act for veſting in Truſtees, certain Lands and Hereditaments at *Weedon Beck*, in the County of *Northampton*, for erecting Buildings thereon for the Service of His Majeſty's Ordnance.

[24th *June* 1803.]

WHEREAS it is expedient to erect Buildings for the Service of His Majeſty's Ordnance in ſome convenient Poſition, and for that Purpoſe to purchaſe the Lands and Hereditaments, Rights and Intereſts herein-after mentioned: And whereas the ſaid Lands and Hereditaments, Rights and Intereſts, are or may be veſted in, or belong to Infants, Femes Covert, Truſtees, or other Perſons, who by Law are diſabled to make any Contracts or Conveyances, in all which Caſes, as likewiſe when any Owner or other Perſon entitled to or intereſted in the ſame, deſigning to obſtruct the publick Service, or to make any unreaſonable Gain to themſelves, inſiſt on extravagant Rates, it will be neceſſary to have Recourſe to the ſame Methods that have been taken in Caſes of the like Nature; to the End therefore that the true and real Value of the ſaid Eſtates, Rights, and Intereſts may be aſcertained, and the Owners and Proprietors thereof, or Perſons entitled thereto, may have a juſt and reaſonable Satisfaction for the ſame, be it enacted by the

60 King's

Act of Parliament 1803 transferring ownership of the Manor of Weedon Bec to HM Government
(courtesy of Weeden Bec Historical Society)

The Royal Ordnance Depot Weedon Bec

The Spur off the Union Canal in the Depot
(courtesy of The Royal Ordnance Depot Weedon Bec Visitor Centre)

Pulley Blocks for standing rigging

The Smithy

Chatham Dockyard

East India Dockyard at Deptford

Mark Brunel's Block Making Machines
(courtesy of Nic Walker)

The Block Mill at Portsmouth
(courtesy of Portsmouth Royal Dockyard Historical Trust)

Carron Iron Works, Falkirk

The Rope House, Chatham

Chapter Six: The Wooden Walls of England
Part I: King Alfred to King Charles II

As an island people, the English have always relied on their ships both to promote trade and to defend our shores. Since the time of the Anglo-Saxon kingdoms, particular attention has been paid to the planting and harvesting of oak trees and their use for shipbuilding. In times of peace, English ships carried their precious cargoes – mainly of wool – throughout northern Europe and into the Baltics and in war defended our shores against attack by Dutch, French, Portuguese, and Spanish enemies. In 1588 Queen Elizabeth's fleet successfully held off a combined Franco-Spanish threat of invasion and by the time of the Restoration in 1660, the Royal Navy – as it was now called – had become England's greatest national institution.

It is not easy to identify the origins of Britain's navy. Some say King Alfred; others King John, but most place its formal organisation in the reigns of King Henry VIII and his daughter Queen Elizabeth I. The former of whom fought the French off Calais and the latter, the Spanish in the English Channel. The modern Royal Navy can be dated to the reign of King Charles II at a time of war against the Dutch empire and to the appointment of Samuel Pepys, the diarist, as Secretary to the Navy in 1666. Pepys was the first individual to provide an intimate picture of its organisation.

It was during the reign of King Henry VIII that the Navy Royal – as it was known until the reign of King Charles II – was first described as the *Wooden Walls of England*, that is, the romantic idea that England was protected by the oak tree, used in the construction of the Navy's ships. The oak tree had been long understood in our history as an icon for the strength and endurance of its people at home and abroad; by land and sea.

King Alfred & the Danes

The Saxons had arrived from the Continent from c. 455 onwards and were described as 'deeming it sport to furrow in British waters, cleaving the sea in a stitched boat' to attack its eastern coastline. Later, in the next wave of invasion, Vikings from Scandinavia raided the country using sleek vessels that were equipped with strong keels, powerful sails, deep, flat hulls of more than sixty feet and large crews. These ships could travel short distances powered by oars, giving them the ability to appear on the horizon without warning. From the 850s onwards, these raids became more frequent; occupations lasted longer and on one occasion a Viking fleet of over 350 longboats attacked London.

The first indication we have of a navy in our national history is derived from the *Anglo Saxon Chronicle* that records that in the summer of 897 King Alfred ordered the construction of a fleet of ships that would be capable of defeating the Danish longboats that had been harassing the Isle of Wight and Devonshire. The ships would be larger than the Danish vessels with up to sixty oarsmen and would be built on the Itchen at Southampton close to Alfred's capital at Winchester. The King's forests in Hampshire would provide the timber required. Alfred ordered his ships to block the mouth of the Exe after the Danes had entered the river and, in a sharp engagement, the enemy's ships were sunk and their crews killed or captured. They were taken to Winchester where they were hung. It is from this engagement that Alfred became known as the founder of the Royal Navy.

William Marshal & The Bayonne

In 1216, the hated King John was forced to sign *Magna Carta* at Runnymede beside the Thames at Windsor. However, he quickly reneged on the agreement and civil war broke out soon after. The barons invited Prince Louis of France to bring an army across the Channel and take over the realm, but in October of that year King John died and the barons changed their minds. Louis had already landed one army in England but this had been defeated at Lincoln by those loyal to King Henry III, aged only nine. Now, Louis planned to re-enforce his troops and sent a large force out of Calais consisting of ten great ships and sixty supply vessels.

In August 1217 William Marshal, young King Henry's regent, assembled a fleet of vessels manned by troops who were promised the plunder from any enemy ships that they captured. The English fleet sailed from Sandwich and intercepted the French as they sailed around the Isle of Thanet towards the mouth of the Thames. Their aim was to take London and restore French rule.

The English sailors approached the French with the sun and wind behind them and launched quantities of powdered lime towards the French ships that choked and blinded their crews.

The French flagship, the *Bayonne,* loaded with troops and stores – and sailing low in the water – was rammed by the English and sunk. The riggings of the remaining French ships were cut and their ships were boarded as they became un-sailable. This was followed by the massacre of their crews and the plundering of their cargoes.

The Battle of Sandwich, as it became known, not only led to the end of French pretensions to rule over England, but also established in the minds of the rulers of Europe, that the Channel represented an insuperable barrier to invasion and that the English had a powerful navy that would defeat any seaborne attack upon its shores.

Henry VIII & the Navy Royal

King Henry VIII was a prolific builder of ships and the architect of the Navy Royal, as it was known in its first three hundred years. His character, well known for its impetuousness, lent itself to grand schemes that included palaces, castles, ships and shipyards. Most of all, he was absolutely determined to get his own back on the French, who, he believed, had usurped England's place on mainland France and in the ancient Anglo-Norman counties of Anjou, Gascony, Maine and Normandy. His request to Pope Clement VII for the annulment of his first marriage to Katherine of Aragon angered all the great monarchs of Europe and initiated the Reformation in England – and later throughout the Continent – that divided Europe for centuries.

The Navy Royal would become Henry's principal means of conducting foreign policy and, ultimately, war. Whilst Henry's first overseas naval campaign ended in failure at the battle of St Mathieu off Brest in 1512, his victory at Flodden Fields against the Scots on land a year later secured his back at home and he now set about building up his fleet.

These events set the scene for Henry's expansion of the Navy Royal and the creation of England's sea power that would end with its vindication in the defeat of the Spanish Armada in the reign of Elizabeth, his daughter, over 70 years later.

Both the size and number of ships increased throughout Henry's reign placing pressure on the manufacture and supply of parts and equipment. Large supplies of timber and iron products were ordered by the shipyards and their overseers including bolts, canvas, chains, paint and pitch. The copper for making guns was purchased from Hansa merchants where it was used at a new gun foundry at Houndsditch.

Henry's demands on the Royal Forest were immense but his depredation of England's abbeys and monasteries between 1536 and 1540, had provided him with a vast supply of timber. At Abingdon alone, the Abbey, that owned 1197 acres of forest, had yielded over 12,000 trees.

Henry plundered not only monastic timber. In 1539 alone he confiscated monastic goods valued at £131,000 much of which was in the form of the lead from monastery roofs along with church plate worth £415,000, including over 900 lbs of gold. By the time the depredations of the Dissolution had ended in c. 1540, Henry and his principal henchman, Thomas Cromwell, *'vice-regent of the King in all matters ecclesiastical'*, who managed the innocently named Court of Augmentations, had amassed a fortune over £420,000 of lands and treasure, much of which ended up in his shipyards.

In 1544, Henry became so anxious about oak supplies that he had Parliament pass an *Act for the Preservation of Woods* that, amongst other regulations, required landowners to leave twelve oak trees per acre standing when they were of 10 inches in diameter or less and less than three foot from the ground. Later, in Elizabeth's reign, these restrictions would be reinforced by prohibiting charcoal making except in the counties of Kent and Sussex, both of which contained many iron forges manufacturing armaments.

Up to his death in 1547, Henry built 70 ships cutting down at least 100,000 trees. In addition to oak, spruce and pine were used for masts; elm for gun carriages and yew for arrows. Oak was a slow growing tree and took between eighty and a hundred years to reach maturity but oak was the tree most favoured by the Navy Royal for its toughness and durability.

The art of shipbuilding and the science of gun founding both underwent significant changes throughout Henry's reign. This meant that ships could be larger and this enabled artillery pieces to be installed in them. The latest of Henry's ships were designed to be floating gun batteries which provided much greater fire power than his enemy's.

It was no longer necessary to board enemy ships to destroy them; the English fleet could stand off and bombard them. Ships still carried large numbers of troops whose task it was to assault; board and overcome the enemy but, in addition, they became purpose-built gun platforms.

The Navy Royal had always consisted of a mixture of ships financed and built by the reigning monarch and civilian vessels lent to the king by private owners in time of war. However, Henry set about creating a fleet of purpose-built warships to take on his enemies. These enemies included England's *auld* enemy, the Scots and, as the sixteenth century developed, France and Spain. These kingdoms were the traditional foes of the English, but now the powerful opponents of England's increasingly bitter Protestant Reformation. For example, James, the King of the Scots, had thirty eight warships and was a constant thorn in Henry's side.

Wool was England's largest export and most important trade at 80% of overseas commerce and, as Europe's greatest producer and exporter, keeping the sea lanes open was a vital strategic interest along with escorting troops on campaigns abroad.

Every year a great fleet assembled off the Isle of Wight to transport trade goods to Bordeaux and return with the wines of the Bordelaise. An even larger fleet sailed from London via Lubeck to St Petersburg with cloth for the Russian Czar before returning home with hides and wax.

Henry's two largest warships were the *Henri Grace a Dieu,* popularly known as the *Great Harry,* a 1000 tons carvel-built carrack (that is, a vessel with two or more masts using a Genoese design) and the *Mary Rose.*

The Great Harry had four masts, was constructed out of 3,739 tons or loads of timber; 56 tons of iron and carried 112 guns of which 51 were large pieces. A revolution in gun manufacture was underway that involved much stronger barrels bound with iron hoops and made in sections that were soldered together. The Mary Rose at 500 tons was smaller and one of seventeen major warships of the fleet. She had four masts and needed no less than nine anchors to hold her.

By this time, docks were in general use on river banks with gates that could be closed and drained by pumps and at the royal dockyards at Deptford and Woolwich shipbuilding facilities were either created or improved.

The Mary Rose had been laid down in 1519 but completely rebuilt in 1536 in preparation for war against France. In the summer of 1545, a French fleet of 225 ships entered the Solent between the Isle of Wight and the mainland carrying an invasion force of 30,000 men, of whom 19,000 were soldiers. 100 ships of the Navy Royal sailed out of Portsmouth harbour watched by Henry himself on land. The Mary Rose was over-laden and as a result her gun ports were close to the waterline. A sudden and violent gust of wind heeled the ship over and she sank within minutes as water poured in through her open ports. The English admiral, Carew and 700 of her sailors went down with the ship. However, the French fleet withdrew.

Henry was devastated by this loss but his attention to maritime strategy and his warship building programme had led to his fleet becoming the most powerful of its age and this would pay dividends for the future defence of the realm.

Elizabeth I & the Spanish Armada

The great innovation of the Elizabethan age was the introduction of the so-called 'race built galleon' designed by, amongst others, Sir John Hawkins (1532-1595). In 1577, Hawkins had been appointed Treasurer to the Navy and for the next twelve years developed this new breed of warships built in the royal dockyards, mostly at Deptford. As a result, when war came, England was prepared for the Spanish Armada that arrived off its southern coast in the summer of 1588.

These new English ships combined speed and firepower that would transform naval warfare. The ships had at least three distinctive features that improved their fighting capability. The first was a longer length with a stepped main deck on which more and bigger guns could be placed. By carrying its guns lower down in the hull, the ship had both more stability and manoeuvrability. The second was the abandonment of the fore and end castles providing a lower superstructure which greatly improved the ship's handling performance by being able to keep its head more closely into the wind. Finally, Hawkins' race-built galleons had tighter and thinner sails that enabled their commander to change course quickly and position the ship more accurately than the billowing, fuller sails of the past had allowed.

At the same time as England's continental enemies had been adding to the height of their ship's castles to facilitate using their smaller guns to fire down onto the decks of enemy ships before boarding them, the English had been cutting gun ports into their ship's sides in order to mount more and heavier guns. Elizabeth's new fleet could now out-sail and out-gun most enemy warships. For example, Drake's warship the *Revenge,* in which he fought the Armada and which had been launched in 1577, carried 34 culverins (lighter cannon) on its fore and aft decks and 30 heavier guns on its upper and lower decks.

In addition to Deptford, ships were also built at Woolwich and Limehouse on the Thames and at Chatham on the Medway. In addition to the new galleons, the Tudor fleet included escorts, guard ships, supply vessels, dispatch boats, tenders launches and transports. In total, ninety-nine warships were commissioned with a further ninety-four assorted armed merchantmen being made available to the Navy by private merchants in times of national emergency. These merchantmen represented the thin line between privateering, piracy and the legitimate trade of the seas which was a feature of the Elizabethan era. They also helped to develop the skills of Elizabeth's renowned captains. The Navy Royal had become a formidable force.

The ships were made of oak using the carvel method, that is, sawn planking was attached to a frame that was formed on a keel. C frames rose each side of the keel to make the frame, rather like the bones of a fish, before oak joints of different types and sizes were added to the frame as it rose to its full height on the main deck. These joints included 'knees', 'futtocks' and 'wales' in addition to the 'stringers' that strengthened the internal frame. The need for oak led to the dockyard shipwrights travelling all over the country to find suitably shaped oak trees.

The King of Spain was involved in a campaign against Protestant rebels in the Netherlands into which England had been drawn. Trade with the Continent had been reduced and King Philip was intent on crushing the rebellion. On the 30th May 1588, a huge armada commanded by the Duke of Medina Sidonia, Philip's High Admiral, set sail from Lisbon. The Spanish fleet was re-enforced with more ships at Corunna before it headed for England where it arrived off the Lizard on 29th July. At dawn on the 31st, the Spanish fleet had reached Plymouth and battle was commenced.

The English fleet that sailed out of Plymouth consisted of 19 Navy Royal ships accompanied by an additional 54 armed merchantmen. These were joined in the Downs off Kent by a further 17 merchantmen. The fleet was divided into four squadrons for ease of command led by the C-in-C Howard, Hawkins, Drake and Frobisher, all of whom were experienced sailors.

The first priority of Elizabeth's fleet was to prevent the Spanish from landing their troops on the English shore and the second was to destroy the enemy's ships. The main function of the enemy fleet was to act as transport for the 20,000 troops who would be landed on the south coast of England. This objective was frustrated by the persistent offshore wind that blew for days and prevented the Spanish fleet from reaching land. The Spanish fleet's offensive tactics at sea were to use a crescent formation to envelop the English ships with its superior numbers and to fight a close action as friend and foe became locked together in combat and the Spanish troops could cross from ship to ship and fight their enemy on deck.

On the other hand, the English fleet needed to stay out of the embrace of the Spanish and to use their superior manoeuvrability and more powerful guns to break through the Spanish encirclement. The English considered that the idea of ramming and boarding was wasteful of life and that it would be their superior guns that would win the day. This meant that the English divisions would need to sail in line, one after another, firing broadsides as they went aiming to break through the enemy's crescent-shaped line. When they were out of range again, they would turn around, reload their guns and sail back through the Spanish ships. It would be the English superiority in gunnery and ship design that would be the most critical factors of the Armada campaign.

The English had never faced such a fleet before and, although superior in numbers at a total of 197 ships compared to the Spanish at 130, no one could know if the English tactics would work. Nor did the English know exactly what the Spanish intended and how they could be stopped. All through August, running battles were fought in the Channel first off Plymouth and then at Portland Bill and the Isle of Wight. The Spanish attempted to keep their original formation of line abreast while the English divisions put in small harrying attacks.

By the beginning of August it was becoming clear that any attempt at landing would continue to be opposed by the English and the Spanish admiral, Medina Sidonia, changed his tactics. He would cross the English Channel towards France and collect more troops stationed in the Spanish Netherlands before making another attempt at invasion.

However, he failed to do so as he had not appreciated the difficulties of sailing the Spanish fleet up the Channel with its dangerous winds and tides and his fleet became the victim of wholly unseasonal weather. His ships were driven towards the approaches to Calais where they were attacked by English fire ships before being caught in the shoals off Gravelines where many of the ships ran aground. Those that remained afloat, now entered the waters of the North Sea in which they were driven further and further northwards.

Although neither side could claim absolute victory at sea, the campaign was an overwhelming victory for Elizabeth and her seadogs. The Spanish failed to land any of their troops on the English shore and the invasion inland never took place. The surviving Spanish ships were blown across the northern-most tip of the British Isles into the Atlantic where wrecks were reported as far apart as Tobermory on the Isle of Mull and at Dunluce Bay on west coast of Ireland where the Spanish warship *Girona* was lost with all hands. Over 1200 enemy seamen were buried in a mass grave outside Dunluce church.

The Spanish beard had been well and truly singed!

Samuel Pepys & the Anglo Dutch Wars

After the uneasy reign of King James I of England and VI of Scotland – who had shown little interest in the Navy Royal – his son, King Charles I, came to the throne. Charles re-introduced the old medieval system of Ship Money by which coastal towns and cities were taxed to pay for the King's ships and started a programme of naval construction with the building of his *Sovereign of the Seas* of 100 guns built at Woolwich in 1637. The Sovereign fought in all three of the later Anglo Dutch wars.

However, in the early Stuart era the Navy Royal's role was diminished and this was the case particularly in the royal dockyards where theft, looting and embezzlement were widespread. Hawkins' *Chatham Chest* was robbed and the contracts for naval stores were sold to the highest bidder, who first skimmed his winnings before selling them on to the Navy. In 1604, it was discovered that Phineas Pett, a Master Shipwright at Chatham, had built a ship for his own use entirely out of stolen government property including its guns, ammunition and stores!

Whilst the fleet had some small deterrent value, in the end, Charles's regime was destroyed by his adoption of a doctrine known as the *Divine Right of Kings* as he clashed repeatedly with Parliament whose Puritan members stood up for their ancient rights of no taxation without the agreement of the Commons and for complete freedom of worship. A long parliamentary battle over many years followed with Charles ruling by Royal Writ until Oxfordshire MP John Hampden, and other colleagues, refused to pay their Ship Money, which had long since been subverted to the King's personal purse.

This was the *cause celebre* of the English Civil War that divided the Nation starting in 1642 and ending with the King being beheaded at Whitehall in July 1649. Initially, the New Commonwealth, led by Protector Cromwell, had little interest in the Navy Royal and was more concerned with fighting on land, invading both Ireland and Scotland. He even appointed *Generals at sea* to emphasise his landward strategies and the Navy Royal was neglected as its remaining vessels were laid up *in ordinary*, meaning that they were anchored offshore of the Royal Dockyards and manned only by a skeleton maintenance crew of a gunner, carpenter and boatswain.

However, the Protectorate was soon obliged to take an interest in its republican Navy and the near seas of the English Channel. Although the Dutch were natural allies – as co-Protestants against both the French and Spanish Roman Catholic empires – commercial rivalry between England and the Dutch Estates was intensifying. The Dutch had almost overcome the Portuguese empire in the East and were challenging the Spanish in the Americas. Competition between the East India Company (EIC, founded in 1600) and the Vereenigde Oostindische Compagnie (VOC, founded in 1602) had become a matter of national interest in addition to clashes in the North Sea over fishing rights and the ubiquitous herring catch, staple of all northern European populations.

Chatham dockyard on the Medway provided the nearest anchorage to the Dutch coast where warships damaged whilst patrolling the North Sea and the Channel could be repaired. From 1649 onwards, almost half the Government's total revenues were spent on the Navy Royal and 190 ships were added to the Fleet. These new ships were commissioned to oppose the Dutch and in May 1652, Parliament passed the first of a series of Navigations Acts which were to be the cause of trouble and strife for the next 200 years. The Act stipulated that only English ships could be used to import goods into the country. The Dutch had large merchant fleets in the North Sea, the Baltic and in the Mediterranean and dominated the *carrying trades,* that is, the carrying of cargo from point to point. The Navigation Acts would destroy this trade.

Ships had become heavier with 42 pounders mounted on the lowest broadside tier of a warship whose guns could now reduce the enemy's hulls to matchwood at close range. On the other decks, 18, 9, 6 and 3 pounders could also do damage as ships closed with one another in battle.

Dutch Admiral Tromp, their leading seaman, tried to run a fleet of over 400 merchantmen escorted by 88 warships up the Channel. Free and unfettered passage was vital to Dutch interests. Initially, the admiral was successful and at the Battle of Dungeness three English ships were sunk. However, in February 1653, the English sank 17 Dutch ships off Portland Bill and in July, General Monck, now serving as a general at sea, defeated the Dutch between Scheveningen and Texel, off the Dutch coast. These were famous victories with the Dutch suffering over 6,000 casualties that included the death of Tromp and with many Dutch ships sunk. This engagement ended the first Anglo-Dutch war.

For the remainder of the Protectorate's life, Parliament's attention was focussed on internal politics with the exception of sea actions against Barbary pirates in the Mediterranean and it was not until the Restoration of the Monarchy in 1660 that renewed interest in foreign policy and, in particular, the dangers of the ascendency of the Dutch in maritime and trade affairs, became of national concern once more.

Charles II had shown an interest in the Navy during his time in exile. Now, prompted by his brother, James, Duke of York, who he had appointed Lord High Admiral of the Navy, the King began to consider the role of the Royal Navy (as it had now become known) as the means to both protect England from her enemies and to project her expanding commercial interests overseas. The merchants of the City of London were desperate to develop their markets and Charles needed the tax take for his high-spending Court.

By his marriage to Portuguese Catherine of Braganza, Charles now had formal access to Tangiers in the Mediterranean and Bombay in India as bases from which to trade. The connection with India would become momentous and would lead to the foundation of Britain's global empire.

Meanwhile, the unilateral seizure of Dutch shipping in home waters in December 1664 caused a second war with the Dutch. James assembled a fleet of 100 ships and 21,000 men who on June 3rd 1665 achieved a stunning victory off Lowestoft with the loss 6,000 Dutchmen killed or captured. However, this was not to be the end of it. In January 1666, France entered the war on the side of the Dutch and in a sea battle off North Foreland in June, England lost three admirals and ten ships including the *Royal Prince.* By the end of 1666, the English were exhausted as London was ravaged by plague and fire and on 7th June Dutch Admiral de Ruyter entered the Thames with catastrophic results.

Eighty Dutch warships entered the Thames estuary; landed troops at Harwich; broke the boom protecting the mouth of the Medway and attacked Chatham. Four of the Royal Navy's largest ships were burned and eight smaller vessels including the *Royal Charles* were taken back to Holland. Only a number of block ships placed across the Thames together with a sunken boom at

Blackwall prevented the Dutch from reaching London. The second Anglo-Dutch war ended in England's complete humiliation at the Treaty of Breda in July 1667.

Three years later in 1670, England and France signed a secret treaty to attack Holland and an elaborate pretext for war was invented. The allied fleets failed to work well together and at the Battle of Texel in 1673, the Dutch managed to split the allied fleets and bring home a valuable convoy from the East Indies. The idea of a joint landing in the Netherlands by English and French troops was thwarted by the opening of the dykes in Zeeland and the third Anglo Dutch ended inconclusively.

In was in this era in the Royal Navy's history, that an individual was appointed to its administration who was to have a profound effect on its long term future as the Nation's *Wooden Walls.* Samuel Pepys had been born in 1633 into a professional family living outside Cambridge. His father was a younger son who had set up as a tailor in London and Pepys was well educated at St Paul's School and thereafter at Magdalene College, Cambridge. Through a family connection, Pepys was acquainted with Edward Montagu, a kinsman of the Earls of Manchester, who was associated with the Protectorate's management of the Navy. Pepys sought Montagu's patronage as his private secretary.

By December 1659, the Protectorate's days were numbered. The Fleet staged the only naval coup in modern history, complaining of lack of pay and poor conditions and sailed up the Thames to threaten Parliament. Meanwhile, General Monk set off with his army from Coldstream with the intention of restoring Charles II to the throne. In March 1660, Montagu sailed by barge down the Thames to take up his command of the Royal Navy accompanied by Pepys as his private secretary.

By May of the same year, negotiations between the Protectorate's Long Parliament at Westminster and the King's representatives in Holland were concluded and the Fleet was dispatched to bring the King home. Pepys was on board Montagu's flagship the *Nasby,* recaptured from the Dutch – and promptly renamed *The Royal Charles* – when the King reached Dover. Subsequently, Montagu was made a Knight of the Garter and an Admiral of the Fleet. Montagu invited Pepys to become the *Clerk of the Acts,* Secretary of the Navy, or more formally, by letters patent on July 13th, *The Clerk of the King's Ships.*

Pepys relationship with the Navy, although sometimes tempestuous, became not only the focus of his professional life but also his passion. It was at this time that Pepys started his near daily diary that recorded in the greatest detail his work of the administration of the Navy but also that of his private, political and social life in the turbulent era of the restored Stuart dynasty that ended disastrously twenty years later in 1688.

The management of the Navy had been chaotic for many years due to the various and often overlapping responsibilities of its officials who were appointed directly by the Monarch. These were usually purchased or given out as royal favours. Often, these office holders knew nothing whatsoever about the sea or of ships and were in it simply for the money. The opportunities for pecuniary advantage were unlimited as the entire budget was sub-contracted to private suppliers of every kind. The Royal Dockyards were an exception to this system but even they had to buy in all the materials that were needed to build a warship and corruption was rife from top to bottom in the royal dockyards.

Pepys was methodical, inquisitive and highly competent. His first action was to become familiar with every aspect of ships and shipbuilding. In 1662 Pepys met Anthony Deane, an assistant shipwright at Woolwich, who not only became a firm friend but also taught Pepys, amongst many other things, the mathematics to calculate the amount of timber required for a ship and how to use a slide-rule for the purpose. This enabled Pepys to challenge the use and cost of timber which marked the start of a life-long pursuit of value for money in the Navy's purchasing procedures. He soon became expert at the sharp practices of naval suppliers and built up a fund of technical knowledge and personal contacts. As Clerk of the Acts, Pepys was responsible for the letting of all naval contracts and was quickly able to make an impression on naval budgets and expenditure.

For example, no records were kept in the Royal Dockyards of the hours worked on ships under construction. As a result there was much scope for deceit. Pepys 's records show the way that his office created registers that recorded every detail of the quality, price and amount of all materials including the purchase of hemp, tar, glazing, hammocks, canvas and masts. In addition, Pepys introduced annual budgets that included the costs of ships under repair and construction and the numbers and costs of the Fleet at sea. In this way, Pepys created a level of trust between King and Parliament that led to major annual revenues being allocated to the Navy. In addition, Pepys almost single-handedly created the world's first industrial complex by investing in management and administrative systems in the dockyards that underpinned every action of the Royal Navy.

One of Pepys's greatest obsessions was the *Chips* system. It was a long-held tradition that shipyard workers had the right to take home the off-cuts, or chips, of the ship building process. This had started, literally, with the chips flying off the cutting and shaping adzes and axes that were used in the forming of the ships' timbers. Chips had now become, by definition, any surplus planking and waste wood that could be carried on the shoulders of one man out of the dockyard gates. The practice had changed from being a harmless perk of the job to a major matter of corruption and theft. Pepys was determined to put a stop to this notorious practice and its abolition epitomised Pepys's attitude to the control of costs.

The three Anglo-Dutch wars between 1652-1674, defined Pepys's work in the administration of the Navy and although on two occasions he was accused, first of corruption regarding the letting of contracts to his circle of friends and, second, of Stuart sympathies beyond the end of that dynasty's time, his work continued. Pepys's contribution to the development of the modern navy was incalculable and, by the time of his death in 1703, the Navy had become the Nation's first truly national institution and Pepys would always be remembered as the *Oracle of the Navy.*

Chapter Seven: The Wooden Walls of England
Part II: Queen Anne to King George III

The mighty oak played the essential part in the development of the most powerful navy that the world had ever seen and by the beginning of the nineteenth century, Great Britain's dockyards and ship-building activities had overtaken those of France, Holland, Portugal and Spain. The Royal Navy inevitably experienced both good and bad times, but the world voyages of James Cook confirmed that Great Britain was the world's pre-eminent power, vindicated by its victory at Trafalgar in 1805.

In the period 1688-1793, from William of Orange's arrival in England from Holland until the outbreak of the French revolutionary wars, the Royal Navy experienced both high and low points. Throughout the eighteenth century, England's industrial revolution had made the nation one of the foremost European nations in continual competition with France, Holland and Spain. England looked to the Royal Navy to protect its traders wherever they might go and to defend the nation against its enemies.

The Royal Navy's campaigns were long and arduous as its warships patrolled and fought across the world. Its activities were located in the Mediterranean, the West Indies, the American coastline, in the Far East and in Asia – a truly global reach. In 1704, the British captured Gibraltar which provided not only a strategic base at the entry to the Mediterranean sea but also the means to control the sea's entry and exit. The following year, in 1705, the British destroyed a French fleet and Sir Cloudesley Shovell attacked and captured Barcelona. In 1706, following up these successes, a string of Spanish ports were taken including Cartagena, Alicante, Ibiza and Majorca. At the same time, on land, the Duke of Marlborough defeated King Louis XIV at the Battle of Ramillies and drove the French out of the Netherlands, so ending the War of the Spanish Succession.

Parliament was generous with its support and naval strength peaked at 228 ships, carrying 9,800 guns and employing over 52,000 seamen. The Royal Navy's reputation was high as Britain's economy, overseas trade, banking and public finances grew. This support extended to the introduction of a number of Acts of Parliament that were aimed at financing the building of forty three new warships from a Land Tax Bill and a Convoy Act to defend British trade. In addition, the organisation of the navy was improved with the appointment of a permanent First Lord of the Admiralty who, for the first time, would be a professional sailor, instead of a royal prince or a politician.

Success & Failure

The main focus for both trade and for eighteenth century warfare, was in the Caribbean and South America, where France and Spain had major imperial and trade interests. The domination of the sugar trade was the greatest prize to be won by the rival nations and advantage swayed back and forth. There were times when the Royal Navy excelled itself, for example, when Admiral Lord Anson (1697-1762), captured a Spanish galleon off Manila in the Philippines carrying a cargo of gold treasure from South America heading back to Spain. When the ship's cargo was paraded through London, thirty two wagons were needed to carry the loot.

However, there were also failures in the Royal Navy's fortunes and the service was not without its problems. For example, in 1707, Sir Cloudsley Shovell sailed a fleet of twenty one ships towards the Scillies where, due to poor navigation, a storm wrecked his flagship HMS *Association,* a 90 gun, second rater on the rocks and 2,000 men died. The disaster prompted the Royal Navy's search for a solution to the problem of longitude.

Throughout the eighteenth century, the names that made the Royal Navy famous throughout the world kept on occurring including Bligh, Boscowan, Cochrane, Collingwood, Hood, Rodney, St Vincent and Vernon, whose names ring down the ages. Admiral Benbow disrupted Spanish shipping in the West Indies but in 1744 at Toulon, a British fleet was defeated; its captains too old and unimaginative and its leader an 81 year old admiral. However, Admiral Lord Anson was not only an outstanding sailor but also a great reformer and realised that success would need to be based on intelligence, secrecy, discipline and supply. He appointed a whole new generation of younger officers who had cut their teeth in the

West Indies under Hawke and led them to success in 1747 at the Battle of Finnistere. Hawke now joined the Western Squadron guarding the Channel Approaches and at the Battle of the Basque Roads, off La Rochelle, his ships sank six French ships with the loss of 4,000 French sailors.

However, in 1755, the Royal Navy suffered an infamous episode when Admiral Byng failed to relieve Menorca with ten ships of the line against a Spanish invasion and was court-martialled and executed by firing squad for cowardice on the deck of his own flagship.

By 1759, the start of the Seven Years War, Britain had a fleet of 275 ships of which fifty-nine were serving overseas with a further 82 in reserve. The campaign at sea was fought across the Atlantic but at the Battle of Quiberon Bay in November 1759 off the French coast, Anson, Hawke and their captains inflicted a decisive defeat on the enemy who lost seven ships. By the end of the war, Britain mustered 301 ship and 85, 000 seamen of which 141 were ships of the line.

By 1778, many of the lessons of the Anson and Hawke era had been forgotten and the Royal Navy was overstretched with its ships stationed too thinly across the world. Admirals Rodney and Hood struggled to overcome a French fleet at the Battle of Chesapeake in September 1781 that contributed to the final defeat of the British in the American war of Independence. This defeat was mitigated in early 1782 by two stunning victories at St Kitts and The Saintes at which the French became disorientated and comprehensively defeated.

Meanwhile in 1794, Hood with twenty-five ships of the line, was hunting a French convoy bringing much needed grain to France from America. At dawn on the First of June, the two fleets locked together and in a fierce battle that lasted all day. Six enemy ships were taken and 7,000 French sailors killed or captured.

At Aboukir Bay in 1798, Admiral Sir Horatio Nelson achieved his first great victory when he annihilated the French fleet and secured the Mediterranean before doing the same at the battles of Cape St Vincent and The Nile

The Press Gang

An issue that was to plague the Royal Navy throughout the 18th century was recruitment. The navy could never obtain the numbers that it needed to volunteer for service in its ships and relied instead on the dreaded *impress.* Impressment, and all that this implied, gave it a lastingly bad reputation throughout the country and especially in port areas, when men were literally snatched off the streets and forced to embark on HM ships about to sail.

Each ship's captain was responsible for recruiting his crew and appointed an officer, usually a lieutenant, to a District on land to manage the Press. This system was not unlike the recruiting districts allocated to the regiments of the Army. Each lieutenant had a *gang,* usually of seamen but sometimes of local toughs, who set themselves up in a local pub and visited fairs and markets looking for victims. The gangs also roamed the streets at night picking up drunks or vagrants. There were generous rewards for officers engaged in the work in addition to a sum of money for each recruit.

Local magistrates found the Press useful for getting rid of trouble makers as well as paupers, vagabonds and petty criminals. The most popular locations for the Press gangs were close to commercial ports where seamen gathered and the chartered companies seamen, in-shore fishermen and Thames lightermen were all a useful source of recruits. Raiding taverns where seafarers were drinking was the standard way of Pressing ashore and on one occasion, when a fight broke out at the Spread Eagle in Tooley Street, Southwark, cutlasses and pistols were used by the Press gang who subsequently found themselves imprisoned for causing an affray.

The Press gang also acted as a naval shore police force, arresting deserters and those who might be hiding them. A riskier but more straightforward way to recruit sailors was whilst a warship was at sea. Commercial shipping could be stopped and searched and seamen forcibly removed. Many a sailor seeing the shores of England for the first time after a long voyage, found themselves removed in a cutter and transferred to a cruising warship going overseas. Cod fishermen returning from Newfoundland, men working herring boats in the North Sea, colliers carrying coal up and down the East Coast and sailors from foreigners ships were all at risk of falling victim to the Press.

Life on board

Life on board ship was dangerous and brutal. Water stored in wooden casks became putrid before it cleared and grew drinkable again. As voyages lasted longer, scurvy became widespread, bread was full of maggots and flour stale. Whilst at sea, food soon became repetitive and indigestible with the bread ration replaced by ships biscuit made from wheat and pea flour supplemented by bone dust which was full of weevils.

Breakfast consisted of oatmeal boiled with animal fat and lunch a pudding made of flour, suet and currants. When meat was available, it was so hard to chew that the sailors carved models from it and after boiling, skimmed its surface to use as waterproofing for rigging. Whilst officers could afford to make private purchases of eggs, chickens and even cows, which they kept in pens on deck, the sailors ate off wooden bowls in messes below decks. Lice and fleas caused typhus and, combined with with scurvy, cost over ninety-thousand lives in the Seven Years war.

Discipline was harsh and a captain who believed that it could only be maintained by the lash made frequent use of it. Beating with a cat-o'-nine tails inflicted severe lacerations on the back with repeated offences being dealt with by the tradition of flogging through the fleet. The most severe offences led to courts martial and ducking, keel-hauling and hanging from the yard-arm of the ship.

Medical care was primitive and ships doctors ministered to a wide variety of injuries that included falls from rigging, masts and sails. Before the discovery of the efficacy of lime to prevent scurvy, doctors had to deal with its affects that included bleeding scalps and gums, lethargy and death. In battle, surgeons attended to horrific injuries including crushing from falling spars and wounds from round and grape shot. The surgeon's saw was his most useful instrument.

In spite of these negative factors, the Royal Navy, whilst perennially short of manpower, still managed to crew its ships and provide a life for its sailors.

Exploration

Throughout the eighteenth century, and alongside the Royal Navy's role in fighting the Crown's enemies, the service also participated in the expansion of knowledge of the world through its sponsorship of voyages of discovery.

These voyages became a speciality of some of its most daring commanders who ventured into hitherto unknown seas, the most famous of which were Admiral of the Fleet Lord Anson who circumnavigated the world between 1740 and 1744 and Captain James Cook, who made three voyages across the Pacific between 1768 and 1780. The names of James Cook and Horatio Nelson remain the two best known names in the long history of the Royal Navy and with good reason.

Cook was the son of farm labourers outside Whitby who learned his trade sailing in uncomfortable and barely seaworthy cogs as they plied their trade up and down the North Sea coast of England carrying coal. Little is known of his early life and the way that he combined his skills in seamanship, navigation and cartography to become the greatest explorer of his age – or of any age. Later, Cook added an understanding of astronomy and mathematics to his repertoire after he joined the Royal Navy as an able seaman in 1755.

In 1758, following the outbreak of the Seven Years War, Cook's ship, HMS *Pembroke,* was dispatched to America to prevent the French from invading Canada and it was here that Cook became a highly skilled cartographer mapping the St Lawrence River and its treacherous shoals and contributing to Wolfe's victory at Quebec.

By this time the Admiralty had appreciated Cook's qualifications and appointed him to command the re-named *Endeavour* fitted out for a major expedition across the Pacific that aimed to discover a continent that was believed to lie to the south-east of India. No man or ship had ever entered these seas and returned safely. *Endeavour* sailed from Plymouth in August 1768 and would only return three years later in 1771. In January 1769, Cook rounded Cape Horn and sailed into the Pacific setting off towards Tahiti.

Ostensibly, the expedition's aim was to observe the Transit of Venus across the southern skies but the Admiralty had another and more secret aim which was for Cook to move further south and explore what was known as Van Dieman's Land, now Tasmania, and New Zealand, which had been touched upon by the Dutch explorer. On the 7th October 1769, Cook's lookout, Nicholas Young, was the first European to set eyes on the east coast of New Zealand. In addition to these aims, Cook had on board a team of scientists led by the botanist Joseph Banks, a prominent member of the Royal Society, whose task it would be to identify the flora and fauna of any newly discovered lands.

Cook now spent the following months sailing around the North and South islands mapping and charting as he went. He was a great namer of his discoveries many of which are familiar to us and amongst which are Hawke's Bay, the Bay of Plenty, the Bay of Islands and Queen Charlotte Sound. Finally leaving New Zealand in April 1770, Cook returned to Van Dieman's Land and, after sighting the mainland, sailed into Botany Bay on the east Coast of Australia, naming it New South Wales, whilst claiming the whole continent as a possession of the British crown,

Cook was running short of supplies and after losing men to disease in Batavia (modern day Djakarta), Cook turned for home, reaching England in July 1771.

It had been an epic voyage of discovery, not withstanding that Cook's expedition had failed to find the mythical Southern Continent. Cook was now a celebrity and regarded by his contemporaries as the greatest explorer and navigator of his age.

Cook's second expedition was even more ambitious than his first. This time, two ships, the *Resolution* and *Adventure* would sail southwards from New Zealand to discover the mythical Southern Continent and explore the vastness of the South Atlantic. In July 1772, Cook left for Cape Town and as he sailed south the weather turned cold and the cattle on board began to die. In January 1773, Cook's ships entered the Antarctic Circle – the first vessels ever known to have done so – and were soon surrounded by icebergs some of which were taller than his ships' masts. In March, Cook turned north-east for New Zealand still searching for the missing continent having sailed further south in the Indian, Pacific and Atlantic oceans than any other explorer.

Cook set in at Tahiti again to replenish his ships stores before returning to Hawke's Bay in New Zealand and sailing south towards the Antarctic for the second time. By January 1774, the *Resolution* was surrounded by pack-ice from horizon to horizon and reached latitude 70° 10' and longitude 106° 34', the furthest south that any person had ever been known to have sailed. Cook did not discover the Antarctic continent as he was too far to its west, but his voyage remains one of the most remarkable ever undertaken. In the summer of 1774, Cook was back in the Pacific and cruising amongst the Polynesian islands before returning to The North Island of New Zealand. In December he rounded the Horn again and started for home. Cook arrived at Spithead on 30th July 1775, after a voyage of three years and eighteen days: the greatest voyage of exploration in British history.

Throughout his time in the Pacific, Cook had experienced a variety of relationships with those he met who were the indigenous inhabitants of Polynesia and beyond. His ships were obliged to put in to shore for many reasons that included making observations of the stars, the collection of flora and fauna, taking possession of territory in the King's name, replenishing supplies and the repair and careening of his ships.

Each of these required a different approach and Cook adopted a variety of tactics to achieve his aims. Sometimes, he was not the first white man that the local population had met. Some islanders could recall positive interactions and others the reverse. For many, however, Cook and his crew were the first white men that they had ever seen and this could be both, deeply troubling or very exciting.

It would be fair to say that Cook's intentions were usually reasonable and practical, but he was a man of his times and when he was not getting what he expected or wanted, his responses could be angry, vengeful and cruel.

For example, often when his sailors made their initial landings they misunderstood the meaning of the welcome they were given and interpreted them wrongly as hostile. This led to shootings followed by reparations. Cook was an easy master of his crew and indulged them ashore but when any of his men deserted, he took hostages until they were returned to the ship. Theft was a perennial problem whenever island visitors came on board and it was Cook's practice to land and pursue the thieves until they were caught and the items returned, taking reprisals as he went. It is impossible to tell the reasons that matters went so badly wrong when he landed at Hawaii on his final voyage. Suffice to say that through a series of both deliberate and accidental misunderstandings, Cook and the islanders fell out with each other with fatal results.

On Cook's third, final and fateful voyage, the aim was very different. The Admiralty were intent on finding the fabled North West Passage that would link the Atlantic with the Pacific and there had already been many attempts made including those of Cabot, Frobisher and Hudson.

Cook would have at his disposal *Resolution* and a new *Discovery,* captained by James Clerke, who had already been twice around the world with Cook. Lieutenant James King, a young astronomer, would be Cook's Second Officer. On 12th July 1776, Cook sailed again for the Pacific arriving back in Tasmania in January 1777. From there, he moved to the Hawaiian islands, that he called the Sandwich Islands – after his patron – and to Hawaii itself. In spring, Cook moved north-east and passed the mouth of the Columbia River and Nootka Sound before reaching the southern shores of Alaska.

This was the most westerly point of the Americas and the nearest point to the Asiatic mainland. From here, Cook moved north through the Bering Straits but soon found himself surrounded by pack-ice that stretched as far as the eye could see. He could not delay longer and as summer ended Cook decided to go south again and make another attempt the following Spring. He left for the Sandwich Islands where his ships would make their winter camp and landed once more in Hawaii.

The Hawaiians gave Cook their usual warm welcome and their chief, Palea came on board. Cook may not have known it, but he was in the process of being deified and his behaviour was under intense scrutiny. On the night of 14th February 1779, Captain Clerke of the *Discovery* reported that one of his ship's boats had been stolen during the night and on hearing the news, Cook immediately planned to go ashore to take hostages until it was returned. When the party landed it was attacked and Cook fired his pistol before being cut down and clubbed to death in hand to hand fighting on the beach.

Cook's body was buried at sea and after Clerke's death, who had taken command, his two ships were brought home by Lieut. James King, arriving in England in October 1780. The Controller of the Navy, Sir Hugh Palliser, Cook's friend and colleague of many years wrote:

> *'He raised himself solely by his merit from a very obscure birth, to the rank of Post Captain in the Royal Navy... He possessed in an eminent degree, all the qualifications requisite for his profession and great undertakings; together with the amiable and worthy qualities of the best men. Cool and deliberate in judging; sagacious in determining; active in execution; steady and persevering in enterprising from vigilance and unremitting caution"*

As Cook had written himself:

> *'I, who had ambition not only to go further than anyone had done before, but as far as it was possible to go.*

The Seven Years War

Naval shipbuilding since the days of King Henry VIII had been focussed on providing warships as gun platforms for use against large fleets in the North Sea and the Mediterranean with their associated command and control systems. Now, as its ships were dispersed across the world in small squadrons, captains of independent mind were required. Capital ships of 74 guns were completely unsuited to global conflict and were not capable of serving far from home or for long periods of time. Smaller warships were required for this new kind of work and more frigates were introduced that mounted 32 guns and were much more manoeuvrable. Pepys had described *HMS Pearl* 'as a speedy and sleek little vessel'.

Sheer numbers alone would not win battles on remote stations and off hostile shores and the newly designed class of French warship, for example, their *Invincible,* a two-decker with only 74 guns, was a much more suitable weapon. When she was captured after the first Battle of Finisterre in 1747 she sent shockwaves through the British naval establishment. She was sleeker, faster, more seaworthy and, most worrying of all, less expensive than her British equivalents.

Anson had been promoted to become Admiral of the Fleet in 1751 and introduced a new class of warship, a 74 gun ship that had the speed and firepower to challenge the French. At the battle of the Nile in 1798, that marked the beginning of the French revolutionary wars, thirteen out of fourteen of Nelson's ships were 74s. Anson also insisted that the Royal Marines should be under the command of the Royal Navy, which enabled it to develop an elite force capable of carrying out amphibious landings.

Between 1756 and1763 the world was engulfed in its first truly global conflict – The Seven Years War – but, by its end, Britain had triumphed over her enemies and for the next 200 years the map of the world would be painted red.

The scale of this war; the operations that were mounted in the farthest places on earth and the logistics that were required to sustain them, was truly astonishing. As was the skill, tenacity and loyalty of the Royal Navy that would be involved in the fight across four continents. The war would be fought by land and sea and the contest would be won by whichever of the protagonists could bring their resources to bear most effectively.

Whilst the war was fought mainly on land, the Royal Navy had a critical part to play in keeping the sea routes open for trade; transporting and supplying the troops who were deployed throughout the world and fighting off the navies of France and Spain at sea whenever necessary.

Britain's increasing industrial strength that had led to its expansion overseas had not gone unchallenged. Both France and Spain were active in the New World; Britain's position in India was insecure and, nearer home, France had gathered over 50,000 troops for an invasion across the Channel which would be launched as soon as the British Fleet could be destroyed.

First, there was a war in Europe. This war was between England, Prussia and the German states on one side and France and its allies, including Austria, Russia, Spain and Sweden on the other. Prussia had become a formidable and highly militarised power led by its ruler, Frederick the Great, and appeared to be a likely ally in the contest that was to come. In the centre of Europe stood the minor kingdom of Hannover from which England had lately drawn its new monarchy. Honour demanded that Hannover could not be abandoned.

France could not be allowed to crush Hannover just as Austria could not be allowed to re-possess Silesia, recently taken by Prussia. Russia stood ready to intervene on one side or the other should her interests be threatened, particularly in Poland. The Mediterranean basin also provided the sea-space for a contest between the Royal Navy and France.

Second, there was a war in the Atlantic as Britain and France struggled to dominate the American continent. England, with its possessions in the North American colonies situated mainly in its coastal states, contested those of France that were concentrated further into the interior and among the river systems that led from the Allegheny mountains into the Great Lakes to the north.

France's ambition in America was to link its possession in Louisiana in the south of the continent with its territories in the north and to create an empire in the New World which would rival Britain's. Britain's task was to prevent the French succeeding in this aim.

Third, both Britain and France already had possessions further afield and had clashed not only in the Atlantic but throughout the West Indies, including Cuba; in the Far East, India, in the Philippines and in Canada. This would be an epic battle for world trade; the domination of the routes to and from rich global markets and for land for both occupation and settlement.

As usual, the war began badly for Britain in all four spheres of conflict. The British Army was a poor instrument. The successes of 1688 and its glorious revolution were long gone and Marlborough's great victories forgotten .

On the European continent, Britain did not have the numbers to defeat France and her allies. In Canada, Montcalm, the brilliant French commander and his American-Indian auxiliaries, captured a British advanced post on Lake Ontario, Fort William Henry and made short work of poorly-led regular British and volunteer colonial American troops. In India, the atrocity of the Black Hole of Calcutta in 1756, made an indelible impression of cruelty on that continent

Despite setbacks, the British dislodged the French from North America at the battle for the Heights of Abraham in 1760 partly due to the excellent co-operation achieved between the commanders of the army and navy that had included amphibious landings outside Quebec that were made possible by the detailed cartographic work of the Royal Navy's James Cook.

Meanwhile, on the European continent, the British won a stunning victory at the battle of Minden in 1759 against a superior

French army. However, the invasion of the British Isles by France remained a threat until November 1759 when Admiral Hawke with twenty-three ships of the line defeated the French fleet at the battle of Quiberon Bay. This put an end to the French invasion threat and not only opened up the Mediterranean Sea to British domination but also led to its command of more distant oceans. Fifty-nine third raters were serving on overseas stations, such as Antigua and Halifax.

Throughout the world, Britain and France fought out the war as the naval and military strength of both countries was stretched to the limit. The Royal Navy was used in India, the West Indies, Africa and elsewhere to harass French interests and frustrate its ability to move re-enforcements around. The Navy also interfered with French trade and threatened France's coastline.

By the end of the Seven Years War France's imperial ambitions had ended and, although there was some exchange of captured territories between Britain, France and Spain at the Treaty of Paris in 1763, peace was now restored until the outbreak of the American War of Independence in 1775 and the French revolutionary wars that started in 1792.

The Seven Years war had radically changed Britain's military and political position.

Britain had started the war with only its American colonies, Nova Scotia, Newfoundland and Jamaica; naval bases in Gibraltar and Menorca; the West Indian islands of the Bahamas, Bermuda and Barbados and its trading posts at Bombay, Calcutta and Madras in India.

By its end, Britain ruled a global empire. Clive and the East India Company ruled India; Wolfe had helped to secure the North American colonies and created Canada. Britain was the undisputed ruler of the waves.

The inexorable rise of the British Empire was only interrupted by its failure in the American War of Independence that started in 1777. Long lines of communications between the Old World and the New, political confusion in London, poor general-ship and enemy tactics for which the British Army was unprepared, led to comprehensive defeat and the loss of the American Colonies.

However, the war had given the opportunity for naval commanders to learn and practice their skills and these would be of inestimable value when the long revolutionary and Napoleonic wars started in 1797 and would be fully vindicated at the Battle of Trafalgar seven years later.

The Revolutionary Wars

France's new generation of warships were equal to much of the Royal Navy's aging fleet and France's well organised marine force specialised in mounting the rigging of its warships and bringing down accurate fire on the enemy's decks below.

The French warships were built for speed whilst the British placed the emphasis on strength when designing its ships. This was because from King Henry VIII's reign, gunnery had always been of primary importance and ships were built that would be stable platforms from which guns could fire. Therefore, the principal tactic of the British was to sail at right angles into the enemy's line and fire off as many broadsides as possible whilst passing through and relying on its skills of seamanship, gunnery and superior command to win the day.

Whilst the French relied on ramming and boarding, the British employed their superior cannons and firepower before the enemy could close with their ships. A particular Spanish tradition was for its gunners to aim at the mast and rigging of a ship rather than its hull. This disabled an enemy ship by bringing down its masts. The Spanish also used chain, grape and canister shot against anyone caught on deck as well as snipers located high in the rigging. The latter would lead to Nelson's death at the height of battle of Trafalgar,

At Trafalgar in 1805, twenty-seven British ships faced a combined Franco-Spanish fleet of thirty-three with the enemy relying on 2649 guns, some 490 more than the British but of lighter calibre. The French were also carrying 30,000 men compared to the 17,000 men in the British ships. The outcome of the coming battle would be down to superior seamanship and the efficiency of the opposing gun crews

Sailing a first-rater ship of the line mounting 120 guns into battle would have been like in modern times a ten-year old trying to steer a supermarket trolley, with only three wheels and laden with shopping, across a sloping and undulating floor as other customers moved up alongside or appeared in front from left and right in its narrow aisles.

The campaign did not start well but the British had an ace up their sleeve: Admiral Lord Nelson, their charismatic and unorthodox commander of the Fleet and hero of the battles of the Nile (1798) and Aboukir Bay (1801). The British had been blockading Cadiz in southern Spain and Villeneuve, the French admiral, needed to draw them off to allow the French and Spanish fleets to combine in the English Channel. This would allow Napoleon to realise his long held ambition to invade England from Boulogne where he had assembled over 100,000 troops and associated landing craft. The British people feared and expected an imminent invasion although the C-in-C Admiral St Vincent had remarked to King George III 'Bonaparte may come to England, Sire, but he will not come by sea'.

Trafalgar

In March 1805, elements of the French fleet sailed across the Atlantic for the West Indies; avoided the British blockade and were followed by a large part of Nelson's fleet. It was a ruse. The Spanish broke the blockade at Cadiz and escaped to sea. The French meanwhile returned to Europe and were now unopposed in the Western Approaches of the Channel.

When the British realised their mistake they left the Caribbean and returned westwards back across the Atlantic but now had to find the French. At first, Nelson believed the French fleet had entered the Mediterranean but on September 29th his scouting ships signalled that the French and Spanish fleets were at sea off the south west coast of Spain at Trafalgar. The British fleet prepared for battle.

Whilst Nelson raised his immortal signal *'England expects every man will do his duty',* followed by *'Close action'* and finally *'Engage the enemy more closely',* the French commander, Admiral Villeneuve, paraded the Imperial eagle around the deck of his flagship *Bucentaure* which was greeted by the response *'Vive Le Emperor'* by all who saw it throughout the French fleet.

The Franco-Spanish fleet was formed into a line with its back to the Spanish coast and throughout the battle this would adversely affect enemy tactics as its commanders looked over their shoulders at their position viz-a-viz the rocky shore. Their situation was not helped by the light breeze blowing in-shore that affected both the opposing navies.

The British meanwhile adopted their historic naval tactic of attacking in line, that is, at right angles to the enemy, in the shape of an arrow strung in a bow. The British attacked in two columns led respectively by Nelson's flagship HMS *Victory* and HMS *Royal Sovereign.* HMS *Britannia* (whose fortunes will be followed throughout the battle) lay sixth in line behind *Victory.* HMS *Bellepheron,* known by the sailors as *Billie Ruffian* lay fifth in line behind the *Royal Sovereign.* She was later made famous as the ship that brought Napoleon from France to England on his way to exile and death on St Helena.

At twelve midday, the column led by the *Royal Sovereign* reached the enemy's line facing the *Santa Ana.* Next came the *Mars* followed by *Bellepheron,* which immediately came under fire from at least five enemy ships. *Victory* cut the enemy's line half an hour later and combat now commenced throughout the Fleet as the massive, lumbering ships of both sides engaged in fierce fighting.

The experience of HMS *Britannia* at Trafalgar typified that of the British fleet.

At first light, all was quiet and *Britannia* was in the process of transferring fresh water from the *Prince,* a complicated manoeuvre at sea.

Before the operation was finished on board *Britannia,* Nelson hoisted his *'Give chase'* order and the battleship struggled to join the line. *Britannia* was one of oldest and slowest in the British fleet and Nelson fretted that she was taking too long, not helped by there being very little breeze to fill her sails and work the ship.

Victory had rushed ahead, her captain eager to reach the opposing line and engage with the enemy. *Britannia* was moving much more slowly and was unable to get up fast. After the battle, there was some criticism of its captain, Charles Bullen, but all of the commanders were doing their utmost.

Soon, *Britannia* was engaged in fierce close combat alongside *Victory, Neptune* and *Temeraire* against the Spanish flagship *Santissima Trinidad*, the latter believed to be the largest battleship in the world. The flagship was putting up a brave fight but was being overcome by the sheer weight of shot coming from the British ships.

On board *Britannia* a young Marine officer witnessed the terrible effect of shot from the *Santissima Trinidad.*

> *'A shot struck the muzzle of a gun and killed or wounded everyone. The shot was a very large one and split into a number of pieces, each of which took its victim. We threw the mangled body of a marine out of the stern port, his stomach being shot away. The gun was split and useless. Amongst the wounded was a man named Pilgrim, who was stooping to take up a shot for the gun, and both his arms were blown off. (Lt. Halloran, Royal Marines)*

Meanwhile, by one fifteen, *Victory* was still in the thick of it and taking most of the enemy's small arms fire as *Britannia* put herself between enemy ships that had not yet fully engaged and a number of British third raters who could no longer defend themselves. By late afternoon, the battle was over and *Britannia* was ordered to pick up survivors from both sides and take them aboard.

On the following morning, the 22nd October, the wind had risen to gale force and securing enemy prizes and putting them in tow had become almost impossible due to the mountainous waves.

As the battle had became more intense, the French Admiral Villeneuve made a fatal mistake when he issued a general instruction to his captains to join the action. The French reliance on such flag orders at this point led to confusion and a subordinate, Vice-Admiral Dumanoir ignored it, waiting for something more precise. The French admiral led five French and Spanish ships away from the fighting and his action became the turning point of the battle. The enemy's Combined Fleet was now outnumbered and wrongly positioned. Less than thirty minutes after the battle had begun, it was lost.

Only one further, and dramatic event was to occur – and the most memorable. The French warship *Redoutable,* commanded by Capitane Lucas, was one of the most disciplined and efficient in the enemy's Combined Fleet. Nelson's flagship, *Victory,* had moved between the stern of the French *Bucentaure* and the bow of Lucas's. This provided the marksmen in the top rigging of the *Redoutable* an ideal field of fire onto the decks of *Victory.* Nelson had never troubled to disguise himself and was fully visible on deck from where he directed the battle. He was shot by a sniper through the backbone at around one-fifteen in the afternoon and died of his wounds shortly after.

Victory – At a Price

After less than four and half hours of battle, the outcome had been decided and there were few French and Spanish ships that had either not been sunk or surrendered. In comparison, not one of Nelson's ships had surrendered and Collingwood, who had taken over command of the British fleet on Nelson's death, put seventeen enemy ships in tow that had been severely damaged or completely disabled.

Meanwhile the gale had turned into a hurricane making the disorder of ships and wreckage a threat to the surviving ships, many of which needed urgent repairs at sea just to keep them afloat. In the French *Redoutable,* of a total of 643 men at the beginning of the battle, 474 were killed and, of the survivors, 70 were seriously wounded.

The surviving enemy ships found some shelter back in Cadiz but ten days after the battle had ended, wounded men from both sides continued to be landed at its port and the shoreline had become cluttered with wreckage and debris. Collingwood began to organise prisoners exchanges and on Saturday 26th October wrote his dispatch that would be carried to England in HMS *Pickle.* On the 2nd November, *Pickle* reached the Channel, sixty miles off the Lizard and arrived at Falmouth the following morning.

Her captain, Lieutenant Lapenotiere, came ashore at once and started the long journey by post-chaise to London. The carriage travelled via Penryn, Truro and Tavistock, before reaching Exeter. Hurrying eastwards through Honiton, Axminster and Bridport, the Lieutenant reached Dorchester and Salisbury before continuing towards London, arriving at the Admiralty after midnight on the 6th November bearing the momentous news.

In his dispatches, Collingwood described Nelson as:

> *'A Hero, whose name will be immortal, and his memory ever dear to his country.'*

Whatever his minor foibles, the memory of Nelson coupled with the name *Trafalgar,* was vindication of the many centuries during which successive rulers and their governments had defended the British Isles against its enemies and in which the *Wooden Walls of England* had played their noble part.

Acorn Flour from Poland

Acorn Bread

Lieutenant James King, RN, FRS, 1750 – 1784

Samuel Pepys 1622 - 1703, Oracle of the Navy

Trenails

Pulley Blocks

The Deed of transfer, the Manor of Weeden Bec from Humphrey Duke of Buckingham to The Provost and Fellows of Eton College 1443
(courtesy of Eton College Archives)

Captain Pemberton's plan for the depot at Weeden Bec
(courtesy of Eton College Archives)

HMS Britannia at Trafalgar 1805

Oak Galls

Medieval Manuscript

Logging

Shipwrights Cuts
(courtesy of Nic Walker)

Chapter Eight *Storeships and Warships*

By the time of the Napoleonic wars, the ships of the Royal Navy and the Mercantile Marine were seen in every port and harbour throughout the world. Many were warships of the Royal Navy that were directly under the control of the Admiralty and its Transport Board but many were owned and operated by the Honourable East India Company and other independent ship owners. The ships of the Royal Navy were commanded by their captains and crewed by sailors serving in accordance with the Articles of War whilst the Transport Board used civilian contractors for the movements of men and supplies.

The Dorah

In June 1815, the Napoleonic wars ended at Waterloo and Napoleon himself was exiled to St Helena, a British-owned island in the South Atlantic. It was described by Lord Melville, the Secretary of the Colonies in Lord Liverpool's government in London as: "Farther away than farther than anywhere else on earth". As far as Britain and the allies were concerned, the farther away the better!

However, this opinion was not universal and there were those both in London and on the Continent who continued to admire the ex-emperor. The authorities were therefore anxious about his continuing ability to make trouble even from that remote spot. In consequence, the government ordered a regiment of Foot to be sent down to guard the island and a squadron of naval vessels to patrol the seas around.

HM 66th Foot (Berkshire) employed two battalions. The first battalion was stationed in India after fighting in the Ghurka wars on the Nepalese frontier and its second battalion was stationed in Ireland after fighting with distinction for six years with Wellington' army in the Peninsular. The Second Battalion was ordered to move to St Helena at once arriving on St Helena in May 1816 where it would be joined by the Regiment's First Battalion in due course when they would be amalgamated to form the island's guard regiment.

The Transport Board was responsible for the movement of troops and supplies to where they were needed. Often, instead of using naval warships, for which there were other priorities, the Board hired ships from contractors including the East India Company. Britain's merchant fleet had increased from 14,500 ships at 1.4 million tons to 22,000 ships at 2.5 million. As the Napoleonic wars had intensified, the search for suitable storeships increased.

In India, the primacy of the East India Company's ships was well established and there were regulations in place to ensure that East Indiamen could only be built in British yards and goods could only be imported in British ships. However, there had always been a *country* trade that shipped goods around India and the Arabian peninsular which was owned and managed in India by Anglo-Indian and Indian merchants. A number of these merchants were also ship builders and there were shipyards in Bombay and Calcutta owned by both British and Indian merchants. Teak was identified as a suitable material from which *country* ships could be built as it does not shrink or splinter. Even better, teak was not subject to worm and lasted longer at sea.

During the Napoleonic wars, when there was a grave shortage of supply vessels, the Transport Board in London hired *country* ships to transport troops around the world and a number of ships for the Royal Navy were built in the dockyard in Bombay, including *HMS Minden,* a 74 rater, built in 1810. The dockyard facilities included a ropewalk and careening facilities that were available to carry out repair work for the Royal Navy's Fleet in the Far East.

A number of such *country* built and privately owned vessels were contracted to the East India Company and carried cargoes to and from England but these were not popular with English shipbuilders and owners.

The *Dorah* was one such ship and had been built by a Bombay yard for F. Edwards & Co. in 1816. She was designed to the latest standards and started plying her trade around India; to and from the Arabian Gulf (Aden, The Red Sea and Suez) and to China. India was increasing its trade in cotton with China in addition to opium and a number of so-called *free* mariners were engaged in the work. Alternatively, there were voyages calling at Malacca and Penang and as far away as Botany Bay and Sumatra.

In 1817 the *Dorah,* storeship, transport and trooper and owned by Edwards or the East India Company, was contracted by the Transport Board to carry the officers and men of the 1/66th from Calcutta down to St Helena. She sailed on the 2nd April 1817 with three hundred men on board.

Such ships were always commanded by a British officer, either from the Royal Navy or the Company's Marine Service, and employed an additional three British officers on board. The remainder of the crew of seventy-five were locally recruited lascars. Rations consisted of salt meat, rice and biscuit and 4,300 gallons of water was stored in oak butts, sufficient for twenty one days at sea. The ship put in at Isle de France, on Mauritius, for fresh supplies. A fire broke out early in the voyage that was extinguished by two lines of soldiers with fire buckets. The Regimental Band played each evening over the following two weeks as they sailed across the Indian Ocean. The party reached the Cape on the 17th June and moved on to reach Jamestown on the 5th July 1817 where the 66th were disembarked..

The *Dorah* was later wrecked in a hurricane off Table Bay, Capetown, on the 4th January 1821. All her crew were saved.

HMS Beaver

Towards the end of the seventeenth century, the Navy Board had invited private shipyards that had not previously built ships for the Royal Navy to tender for the work. *HMS Beaver,* fourteen guns, was built by Robert Inwood & Co. at Rotherhithe in 1761. She was classed as a *Brig Sloop,* had no forecastle or quarterdeck and carried either two or three masts with square rigged sails. The design of brigs had been adapted from merchant ships and they were armed with between 10-16 carronades. By 1814 there were 181 brig sloops in the Fleet. Brigs had a number of uses that included taking part in coastal blockades in the English Channel, for example, outside Boulogne and Dieppe and on convoy duties and message carrying across the Atlantic and in the Mediterranean.

At the end of the Napoleonic wars in 1815, there was no longer the need for the employment of almost six hundred masters and commanders, in the rank below captain, who competed for the command of less than the two hundred sloops and brigs remaining in service..

Frederick Marryat (1792-1848) the son of a wealthy London merchant joined the Royal Navy as a first class volunteer in 1806. Marryat had made his name in the Napoleonic wars as a daring young officer serving under Captain Lord Cochrane, the notorious *sea wolf*, who had made himself famous for his cutting out operations against the French in the Mediterranean and the attack using fire ships in the Basque Roads. As a young midshipman, Marryat had commanded one of the fireboats that had caused chaos amongst the French fleet at night that had led to their being wrecked against the rocky shore. He had taken part in the coastal blockades outside Boulogne, Dieppe and Fecap that bottled up the French fleet and was also known to be a strong swimmer. On a number of occasions he had rescued sailors who had fallen overboard. Now the war had ended, Marryat was on half pay and unemployed before his father used his influence at the Admiralty to secure his son the command of a ship. By the time that Marryat took over command in June 1820, *HMS Beaver* was long past her best.

While still in the rank of lieutenant, as the ship's master and commander, Marryat had almost unlimited powers in his first independent command. He experienced no difficulty in recruiting his crew at Portsmouth due to high unemployment in the post-war period and was piped aboard *HMS Beaver* on the 27th September 1820.

The captain of one of His Majesty's ships was a combination of monarch, judge of the supreme court, and its jury. There was no appeal from his sentence and his word was absolute. This worked well if he was competent and a stable personality but was disastrous if he was violent or a martinet. Then, the crew suffered; the ship became a floating hell and the threat to good order and discipline from mutiny was ever present. Marryat served under both good and bad captains and was determined that he should be known to his men as fair.

The captain was responsible for the muster book that recorded the personal details of the crew including their tattoos that could be recognised if they deserted. He allotted his crew to their duties; kept the keys of the magazine and exercised the guns. The captain wrote up the daily ship's journal in duplicate, one for the ship and the other for the Admiralty. He was responsible for all stores and for keeping the ship properly ventilated. He took three eighths of prize money and, as Marryat had learned from Thomas Cochrane, his wartime commander and hero, this activity could often become the primary occupation of the ship and make her captain and crew rich.

HMS Beaver proceeded on the long voyage into the South Atlantic. Passing Madeira and Tristan d'Acuna, she reached Jamestown, the capital of St Helena, in March 1821 after 256 days at sea where he joined the Royal Navy's Island Squadron.

The situation on St Helena was complicated. The ex-emperor, Napoleon Bonaparte had fallen out with the governor Sir Hudson Lowe long ago and they had not met face to face for three and a half years. Napoleon continued to fantasize of being rescued and joining his brother Joseph in the United States of America or being declared the liberator of a Spanish colony in South America. It was ironic that Marryat's last commander, Cochrane had been appointed commander in chief of the newly formed Chilean navy fighting against its colonial ruler, Spain.

For a long time, there had been rumours in London and elsewhere that a rescue attempt would be mounted from either Baltimore or Buenos Aires. An American brig *The Damned Yankee* was in the habit of coming towards the island flying British colours to confuse the guard Squadron before raising the Stars and Stripes and sailing away again. There had even been a plan to rescue Napoleon using Robert Fulton's submarine, the *Nautilus,* that would land a beach party; raid Longwood House, where Napoleon was imprisoned and carry him to freedom.

The Island Squadron was kept busy by maintaining an exclusion zone around the island. St Helena was contracted by the British government to the East India Company as a staging post for its shipping to and from India and there were often up to thirty ships anchored offshore while the replenishment of their stores took place. Now, an exclusion zone had been introduced and no shipping could approach Jamestown until it had been boarded and its cargo inspected by the crews of the Squadron.

However, soon after Marryat had arrived in March, Napoleon's health deteriorated and he died on the 5th of May 1821. Marryat was already an accomplished amateur artist, sketching popular caricatures of shipboard life that had been engraved and published by George Cruikshank in London and had even come to the attention of King George IV. Now, he was asked to draw the emperor's death mask and sketched a profile of Napoleon lying on his death bed that was dispatched to London the following day along with the news of the tyrant's demise.

There was no further use for the Island Squadron and Marryat sailed for home. Marryat's career in the Royal Navy was not quite ended and he served in the Far East during the Burmese war before retiring to Norfolk where he wrote a series of successful novels including *The Children of the New Forest,* a romance of the English Civil War.

Chapter Nine: Three Giants of Industry Observed

The logistics of empire required an immense effort of management and administration across four continents. Great Britain fought a global war that required troops and supplies of every kind to be delivered from Great Britain to as far apart as Canada, the Caribbean, the European continent and Iberian peninsula, India and the Far East and the United States of America. At the beginning of the conflict, the Government's organisation was fragmented and relied on a myriad of sub-contractors but it soon became apparent that this would be insufficient against a determined enemy. The Nation had already experienced a revolution that had placed its industry at the forefront of invention and innovation and these changes were now harnessed to fight the 19 long years of war. The great sites at Chatham, Portsmouth and Weedon Bec exemplified the Nation's war effort and were the locations of its most advanced industrial efforts.

The Royal Dockyard – Chatham

The Royal Dockyard at Chatham was the British Navy's dockyard *par excellence* and primary defence base for over three hundred years. Chatham was the largest employer in England and probably, in the world. Chatham developed all the intricate and vital workforce skills that enabled it to build, launch and repair the mightiest of ships, the most famous of which was Nelson's *HMS Victory* whose keel was laid at Chatham in 1759.

Chatham lay close to the capital and the English Channel; the river Medway's muddy banks were washed regularly by the tide and its sloping edge could be used to draw up ships onto their sides where they could be *graved.*

The *Christopher of the Tower* was the first ship to be fitted with guns in 1410 and the earliest record of a Chatham-built ship was the *Henry Grace de Dieu,* better known as the Great Harry, ordered to be built in 1488 by King Henry VII. She was the first ship of the Royal Navy with one mast and one sail. Later, in the reign of

King Henry VIII, another two masts were added and her name was changed to the *Regent.* At the time, local trees from Kent and Sussex were grown and marked for felling; Spanish iron was forged for chains and nails and sawyers worked in saw pits to form the ship's planking and decking. After launching the Great Harry was anchored close to shore.

Whilst some of the Royal Navy's ships continued to be built at Deptford, Chatham became not only a dockyard but also a naval base with generations of sailors and marines stationed in and around the port. By the time of Queen Elizabeth's reign, the naval establishment had its headquarters in Chatham and the dockyard became the chief yard with investment in its cranes and the first of its graving docks.

The first ship to be accommodated in a dock with its entrance sealed by a dam was the *Eleanor,* a royal barge used on state occasions. Mud dams that had to be broken up every time a ship came in or out of dock, were soon followed by timber-built dry docks with hinged gates. By1581, Chatham, with its permanent wharves and storehouses was by now the largest of the Government's dockyards and exceeded the combined capacity of Deptford, Portsmouth and Woolwich. At this time, one of Queen Elizabeth's favourites, Sir John Hawkins, was responsible for the dockyard as the threat of invasion by Spain came closer.

Hawkins became one of the principal architects of victory through his innovations in ship design and his joint command of the Fleet during the Armada campaign of 1588. After the battle Hawkins created the *Chatham Chest,* into which all serving sailors paid a monthly amount from their wages for the relief of their destitute colleagues.

The Stuart dynasty, that followed the Tudors, were less interested in the nation's Fleet and in the reign of King Charles I, of a total number of forty three naval vessels, seventeen were unserviceable. However, during this time a new dry dock, two masts docks, a rope making shed and a sail loft were built to undertake the increasing work of the dockyard. During this era, debts were left unpaid and Cromwell's parliamentarian government owed over £1 million to the dockyard's contractors for materials and wages.

By 1690, the victualling and supply of all HM ships had also become the responsibility of Chatham and additional warehousing was built to hold stores that included a slaughterhouse, bakery, brewery, oar makers and painters shops.

In 1694, the role and importance of a marine force that served on board the Navy's warships was recognised in the formation of the Royal Marines based at Chatham.

Chatham dockyard now occupied an area of 65 acres with four dry docks and by 1786, 604 qualified shipwrights worked in the yards alongside other trades including sailmakers, riggers, anchor-smiths, caulkers, mast makers and scavel men. Scavelmen were unskilled workers who assisted the shipwrights in cutting the ships' timbers, maintained the dockyard; pumped water out the docks and moved the ships' timbers around.

The Mould Loft at Chatham was the largest of its kind in England and its floor could accommodate first the paper drawings and then the battens for the design of three warships simultaneously. In 1995, the main timbers of HMS *Namur,* launched at Chatham in 1756, were found lying intact beneath the floor of the old Wheelrights Shop. The ship was broken up in the nineteenth century and perhaps had been placed there intact as a permanent memorial to the traditions of the dockyard's wooden world.

Roperies were of particular importance where hemp was stored and worked before being spun and tarred. In 1790 a new purpose-built three-storey ropery was built that was, and remains, the longest in the world at 1140 feet in length, or a quarter of a mile. The hemp fibre was imported mainly from Russia and was first *hatchelled* or combed before being spun into various types and sizes of rope. For example, by Admiralty regulation, anchor rope had to be a minimum of 740 feet in length. Riggers mounted the masts (using standing rigging shrouds or ropes) and sails (using running rigging). A 74 rater used 48 tons of rope that stretched 30 miles, end to end.

The dockyard's smiths worked in constant heat as iron bars were welded together on the forges to form the vertical stem (shank) and lower blade (fluke) of the anchors that could weigh up to four tons in addition to other iron parts and its millwrights carved and assembled sailing blocks by hand.

Throughout the eighteenth century, Chatham retained its premier position with dry docks that could build four ships simultaneously compared to a total of five docks between the other three docks in

England and no less than four of the principal warships at Trafalgar originated from Chatham: *HMS Victory, Revenge, Temeraire* and *Leviathan.*

In addition, a number of hulks lay offshore that were used to house recruits who had not yet been sent to sea; keep prisoners of war secure and lodge stores. There were also a number of sheer ships, that is, ships that had been stripped down to their decks and had had cranes installed that could lift heavy loads on board, for, example guns and masts.

It took fifty shipwrights to build a 74 rater and in addition, there were 90 caulkers, 80 carpenters and 240 labourers on the job. A total of 1647 staff worked at Chatham. In 1793 the work of the dockyard had been expanded to 1,800 staff as preparations for war continued and more vessels were brought out of *ordinary* (storage) which had to be surveyed, re-coppered and rigged at the same time as twenty more ships were commissioned amongst which were *HMS Terrible* (1762), *Vengeance* (1785), *Audacious* (1785), *Medusa* (1801), *Hermione* (1782) and *Suffolk* (1775) each of which were to play their part in the war and were emblematic of Chatham's exceptional contribution to its conduct.

However, in the nineteenth century the focus for the Royal Navy's operations moved to Portsmouth and Chatham on the Medway was no longer considered a suitable location for warship building although submarine construction continued until 1964 when the last naval vessel was launched from the yard ending 300 years of service.

The Block Mill – Portsmouth

The Block Mill built inside the Royal Navy's dockyard at Portsmouth is amongst the most remarkable buildings in Britain: The Mill is the location of the world's first ever in-line, automated production line and ushered in the age of mass production using machine tools. Inside, the now dilapidated, No. 5 warehouse, Marc Brunel (1769-1849), built a line of 45 metal machines to manufacture wooden sailing and pulley blocks.

Up until that time, the production of pulley blocks had either been subcontracted to a firm in Portsmouth or made in the royal dockyards. At the time, Portsmouth Dockyard was undergoing significant development under the guidance of its chief designer and engineer, Sir Samuel Bentham (1757-1831), the Inspector General of Naval Works, one of whose principal contributions was the introduction of steam driven machinery. A number of engine sheds were built, housing engines powered by coal that produced steam to turn shafts that drove belts attached to machinery. The first of these in the dockyard was used to cut wood into planking for decking and other purposes. Bentham, an inventor himself, was sympathetic to Brunel's ideas and the two men worked well together to adapt and develop the machinery that would be installed in the Mill.

The actual machines, of which there would be forty five in all, would be built in London by the engineer Henry Maudsley (1771-1831), the inventor of the world's first machine tools with their inter-changeable parts that could be used for the manufacture of variously sized screw threads. Bentham's, Brunel's and Maudsley's truly innovative idea was that the machines at Portsmouth would be made out of shaped and cast iron parts screwed together.

Fourteen different machines were designed to make the shell, the sheave and the pin of each block and these included pendulum, corner, crown and circular saws; boring, broaching and mortising machines; coaking, shaping and scoring engines; riveting hammers and a face-turning lathe.

The most critical part of the block was the *sheave* or cog wheel through which the sheet would be passed. The sheave was made of *lignum vitae,* the hardest wood in the world that was imported from South America and cut by a machine saw in the Mill.

Brunel was paid for his invention on the basis of the annual savings that the dockyard would make by the mechanisation of the pulley making process. By 1808, unskilled labourers had replaced the skilled men in the Block Mill and were producing 130,000 blocks annually. Brunel's payment amounted to £21,174 12s 10d.

The site of the Block Mill was also of significance. The building was erected over a large sump that was used to drain sea water out of one of two docks that were a part of the original dock basin built in the seventeenth century. A tunnel let the water out of dock and into the sump which was at a lower level to the dock and could emptied out using a horse powered pump.

The open sump was now covered over by the construction of vaulting and the Block Mill was built at ground level above the sump. The roof of the Mill building was held up by two columns of wood-turned pillars designed by Bentham using one of his wood-turning inventions. A separate engine room was built at one end of the building and the steam generated drove a shaft along its whole length. From this shaft, individual belts were run off to each machine which lay either side of the central shaft in two lines.

In August 1802 the Admiralty approved the work and the block making machinery began to be manufactured. In January 1803, the medium sized block line was installed followed by the smaller block line in May of the same year. By September 1807, there was sufficient machinery to supply all the needs of the Royal Navy.

Whilst block making itself was of limited interest, Brunel's machinery at Portsmouth became world famous as the location of the world's first ever automated, in-line, mass production manufacturing facility using machine tools made of metal. In time, this would introduce production technology that would power Britain's second industrial revolution throughout the nineteenth century.

The Royal Ordnance Depot – Weedon Bec

The Manor of Weedon Bec outside Northampton – and almost in the centre of England – remained unaffected by the Industrial Revolution until a proposal was made for the construction of a canal to be built on its eastern edge. This was the Grand Union Canal between Birmingham and London, via Watford, with branches to Leicester in the north and Oxford in the south. Now was the time when the development of the canal system along with the extraction of coal and the invention of the steam engine were revolutionising Britain's economy and society.

The evidence for the canal's future economic success was clear in the reduced freight rates that its owners charged. A 280lbs. sack of flour cost 4s 6d by road between Reading and London but by barge the cost was reduced to 6d. Now, Britain had a national network of sheltered and accessible coastal waters and navigable rivers and canals when compared to its enemy France. By 1800 the canal system had given the country a highly significant logistical advantage over the enemy as supplies for the Army and Royal

Navy could be shifted quickly throughout the canal system into its network of depots at ports and dockyards throughout Britain.

Weedon Bec was already well situated for industrial development with two turnpikes running through the Parish and the village became an obvious target for canal investors and owners who eyed its lands with envy. In 1799, at the outbreak of war, the government needed to both improve and increase the administration of its military supply lines and stores. Weedon Bec looked like a suitable location for a new centralised supplies organisation.

A proposal was made that Weedon Bec should be joined to the Grand Union by the construction of a spur and the work was put in hand. In 1803, an Act of Parliament was passed that confirmed its transfer from its owners to the government for industrial purposes and by 1804 plans to erect a barracks and factory had been agreed. A Captain Pemberton of the Royal Engineers was instructed to make plans for its construction. The original area for development would be 53 acres later expanded to over 159 acres. In addition to the eight storehouses, a number of residences for senior officers were planned together with a barracks for 500 men. The storehouses could hold 200,000 small arms and gunpowder magazines, separated from the storehouses and surrounded by earth blast banks, were filled with ordnance and ammunition.

The warehousing built at Weedon were a prime example of early nineteenth century industrial architecture. Eight, large two storey buildings each measuring 160 x 35 ft. were constructed either side of the canal spur and goods were loaded and unloaded by crane and moved on wagon tracks directly into the buildings. The upper stories kept small arms and lighter supplies and the ground floor heavier and larger items such as field guns. A basin halfway up the canal enabled the barges to be turned and fortified gatehouses were built either end of the spur to provide security. Thick walls with bastions at each corner were built around the whole depot complex.

The site was defended against attack by a battalion of infantry, a squadron of cavalry and a troop of horse artillery and at the time of an invasion threat by France, King George III planned to move into the Depot as the furthest defended location from the English Channel.

In 1809 it was reported that an order from the Ordnance Board for the delivery of 22,000 muskets and 120 artillery pieces was fulfilled in 48 hours for delivery to London Port by canal barge.

For the next 150 years essential military supplies were distributed from Weedon into British ports and carried in storeships for the Transportation Board supplying forces who served by land and sea throughout the world. The theft of supplies was an ever present threat and whenever soldiers' boots were dispatched only left or right boots were shipped on a vessel so that potential thieves could not make up and sell a full pair. As a result of the development at Weedon, the population of the village and its surroundings increased from c. 600 to 2000 with over 600 labourers working in the complex.

Chapter Ten: The Mighty Oak

The Mighty Oak is the best known tree in the forest. The oak tree produced fruit that fed ancient people and animals; its timbers could be cut, sawn and carved for use in a wide variety of settings including barns, boats and ships; its bark was used for tanning and its galls for making ink. Most importantly, the oak tree provided the timbers for the Royal Navy's ships, the Nation's greatest national asset, that was always known as the Wooden Walls of England.

Throughout the history of England – and later Great Britain – the oak tree has played a significant part in the nation's prospects and its cultural, industrial and natural associations are woven into many aspects of our island' story.

From the earliest of times, the oak tree formed the basis of the extensive woodlands and great Royal forests that covered much of the land and from which the population drew both its inspiration and its resources.

The oak had multiple uses and was the most favoured material for human use, not least for boat and, later, ship building.

England relied on its foresters, boat builders, shipwrights, sea captains, navigators and seafarers for both its trade and defence and all of these in turn depended on the timber of the mighty oak.

As a result, oak trees and oak forests became a precious resource for the nation to be cultivated, protected and harvested with care.

As seaways became more accessible and trade became a key economic activity, skiffs, barques, cogs and ships became a common sight in ports, harbours and river mouths throughout the nation's coastal areas. In addition, slips and docks and the means to design, build and launch ships became a universal activity that required essential skill and employed thousands of men and women.

Alongside the many uses of oak for trade and domestic use, England's kings and queens not only owned and managed much of the nation's stocks of oak trees and timber, but also kept a special place for oaks that went beyond the building of their royal halls and palaces to include their naval vessels and fleets.

The adaptability of oak lent itself to the construction of the royal fleet with which the reigning monarch would protect the nation from invasion by hostile forces and project the power of the kingdom. The Navy Royal of King Alfred and subsequent rulers became known as the *Wooden Walls* of England capable both symbolically and in reality of defending the realm from attack.

The investment made in warship construction was the greatest that England's kings and queens made in every reign and although the industry was often blighted by corruption, shipbuilding both commercial and naval became the most advanced industrial activity in the land.

In its heyday and as England's influence spread across the globe, more and more ships were required to carry goods across the oceans and to defend the convoys in which they were carried. Competition with Portugal, Spain, the Netherlands and latterly France only accelerated this impulse until Great Britain found itself at the very centre of global politics and trade.

Alongside the planting, growing and harvesting of oak went the skills of the ship designer and the shipwright and the myriad of skills needed to lay down, construct and launch ships. The number and parts of oak used in shipbuilding were all carefully calculated both in the forests where the oak was grown and cut and in the workshops of the naval yards where oak was formed and shaped. It took several years to build a ship and each stage of its construction was critical for its future success. Decaying or ill-fitting parts would lead to its early end either fetched up on the rocks in a violent storm or lost in a battle at sea.

England's first great industrial revolution that had been inspired by the use of coal and the invention of steam-driven machinery had promoted equally important developments in her shipyards where ideas for the mechanical handling and cutting of ship's timber were introduced.

Another profound change had been the manufacture of ships' pulleys made of oak using in-line machine tools at Portsmouth. This invention, introducing the world's first ever automated in-line production facility would become the standard method of manufacture throughout the industrial world.

The nation's prosperity, both civil and military and its defence, housing, livelihood and trade all depended on the oak tree and its multiple uses.

Acknowledgements

Once again I should like to thank Nic Walker, my (almost) daily walking companion, who endured many hours of *futtocks* and *frames;* joined me on our expeditions of inspection to Chatham, Portsmouth and Weedon Bec and made valuable comments on the text. Nic Also took many of the photograph that accompany the text.

My thanks to Asa Britt and Nigel Bradshaw, old family friends, with whom my wife and I stayed in Sweden, that enabled me to visit the Marinmuseuam at Karlskrona where I learned more about ships and ship building.

My thanks to Dennis Miles and Grahame Willcocks, respectively Chairman, and Vice Chairman, Portsmouth Royal Dockyard Historical Trust who arranged our visit to Marc Brunel's Block Mill in the yard and for the use of the Trust's photographs. The latter is the only qualified naval shipwright that I am ever likely to meet!

My thanks to Julia Johns of the Weedon Bec History Society for key information about the site and to Steve Larner at the Royal Ordnance Depot Weedon Bec Visitor Centre for his photographs. Also to Georgina Robinson, Archivist, Eton College, who opened up the Eton archives for me where I spent an exciting and informative day and for the use of the College's original documents.

My love of history comes from my grandfather, Henry Verey DSO, (HEV) who served with the British Army in World War I in Flanders and in Italy on the Piave. I also owe an enduring debt of gratitude to Sir Robert Birley, late headmaster, historian and educationalist who once preached at Evensong in Eton College Chapel on the theme of Lanfranc and the Abbey of Bec. I have been reminded of his sermon over sixty years later and of the connection between Eton and Weedon Bec.

Finally, my thanks are due, as always, to Iola my beloved wife of fifty-five years, whose patience with my urge to write has been wonderful to behold.

About the author

Michael Fass was responsible for one of the largest community-based economic development organisations in the UK. He was educated at the universities of Cambridge, Edinburgh and Lampeter and was ordained in 1995 serving as priest-in-charge at Rosslyn Chapel, Midlothian, for nine years whilst continuing to work in community development in the UK and throughout Europe. He was a founder director of the Prince's Scottish Youth Business Trust and has chaired two UK national charities.

He now lives in Herefordshire and teaches at the universities of Gloucestershire & Manchester. In 2016 he published *Salute Me When You See Me* an affectionate portrait of the father he never knew who was killed in action in Normandy in June 1944. The book was based on his earlier 1994 BBC film, *Relative Losses.* In 2020, Michael published his first historical fiction adventure novel, *Napoleon's Drop,* which told the story of Napoleon's escape from imprisonment on St Helena in Robert Fulton's submarine, the *Nautilus.* Michael has also written a factual account of the ex-emperor's exile on St Helena. He is a Fellow of the Royal Historical Society (FRHistS); has been married to Iola for fifty-five years and has three children and seven grandchildren.

The author curates the website www.napoleon-on-st-helena.co.uk

Appendix 1
Weedon Bec & Eton College

Eton College owned the manor of Weedon Bec between 1445 and 1803. The land had been granted to the College by Humphrey, Duke of Buckingham, formerly Earl of Stafford, who was a close advisor and member of King Henry VI's (1421-1471) Council. The King had founded Eton – *Collegium Beate Marie de Etona* – in 1440 and needed capital and income to sustain his investment. Henry could see the buildings going up in Eton from his home at Windsor Castle and he took a particular interest in the seventy poor scholars who would live and learn there.

Weedon Bec had been the property of the kings of England from the time of William the Conqueror who had gifted the manor's income to the Benedictine Abbey of Bec, at Le Bec Houllouin, in Normandy. Lanfranc, the Abbey's Italian abbot, was a noted European scholar and Duke William had appointed him to be his first Archbishop of Canterbury after the Norman Conquest in 1066.

The English lands of Bec became known as *alien priories* because of their Norman ownership and the duty that they owed to their mother house. Alien priories included those owned by the Benedictine, Cistercian and Cluniac orders located throughout England. Bec's property was extensive and included four priories, five granges and over twenty manors and other churches, titles and pensions. The earliest of these had been granted to Bec in 1133 (Ogbourne St George and St Andrew) and subsequently others were given over by successive Anglo- Norman kings and nobles as the result of their bequests to commemorate their forbears or as a specific act of devotion..

The first written record of Weedon Bec's ownership by an English monarch is dated 1305 alongside others including those at Cowick, Goldcliff, Ogbourne, Stoke-by-Clare and Tooting. The prior at Ogbourne was the senior officer of the Bailiwick of Bec in England and carried out regular visitations on behalf of the Abbott of all the other Bec properties scattered throughout England. However, hostilities between donors broke out regularly as kings, bishops and secular patrons struggled for supremacy and the rights of presentation. In general, the monks and priors of Bec led quiet and uncontroversial lives managing their beef stock, dairy herds and sheep flocks and were well known for the quality of their cheese.

The main task of the English houses, in addition to their duty of intercession for their original donors, was the management of their lands to provide an income for Bec. This included the sub-letting of property and the granting of leases for land and revenues from fisheries, mills and woodlands. This work was overseen by a series of stewards, bailiffs and reeves who held regular manor courts that resolved disputes

By the beginning of the fifteenth century the connection between the Abbott of Bec in Normandy and the Abbey's English estates had been lost through the long hundred years of warfare between England and France and many were in decay or ruined. The manor at Weedon Bec had long before reverted to the king and in 1439 Buckingham was granted the manor by King Henry VI by enfeoffment, that is, through bypassing the usual legal restrictions on the transfer of property and providing certainty of possession. However, this was clearly a device. First, Weedon Bec was left to Eton in Buckingham's will and then, shortly afterwards in 1445, he made the manor over to Eton, its ultimate destination, in perpetuity.

Henry VI (1421-1471) was perhaps the most problematic ruler in England's long history. He was born shortly before his father, King Henry V, of Agincourt fame, died of poisoning in France. Henry V had been a great warrior whose bravery would sound down the ages but his career compared ill with his son's, the infant heir who was brought up at court by Henry V's widow, Queen Catherine of Anjou.

The boy was dreamy, kind, loved his books and was fascinated by the rituals of the Church;

'I would prevail if prayers might prevail,
To join your hearts in love and amity.
Civil dissension is a viperous worm
That gnaws the bowels of the commonwealth.'

(William Shakespeare, Henry VI, Part One, v68/72)

He was interested in the ways of learning and the promotion of peace through education; hence his sponsorship of his two favourite foundations at Eton and at King's College, Cambridge. However, what the realm needed was strong and decisive leadership as the two principal noble factions of York and Lancaster struggled for the domination of court and country.

The nobles did not take kindly to Henry's unworldliness when he allocated titles and land to different individuals on consecutive days and as his treasury quickly became depleted due to his boundless generosity to his relatives and friends.

A principal cause of trouble was Henry's long struggle with his arch rival King Philip of France. Following his father's success, England ruled large parts of France up to and including Paris in an alliance with Philippe of Burgundy, France's other principal enemy. In particular, Maine and Normandy had been English possessions for over 300 years and needed constant attention as the French king raided towns and cities along its borders. Henry was not prepared to join the field of battle himself but relied on his appointed commanders and always owed arrears of wages to his soldiers. Soon, both of the historic lands were lost to Brittany and France for which Henry was never forgiven by his nobles.

England had already suffered the experience of a divided nation in an earlier civil war caused by the struggle over a disputed inheritance that had led to the Barons War (1215-1217). The certainty of the line of succession had been disputed ever since then and now rival Yorkist claims led to endless disputes that weakened Henry's already enfeebled rule.

It did not help that at a critical time in his reign, Henry contracted melancholia and was put out of action suffering from depression while his mother tried to hold back rebellion. Eventually it was too much and after a series of battles, including Towton in 1461 at which the Lancastrian nobility was destroyed, Henry was captured and imprisoned in the Tower of London while a rival Yorkist, Edward IV, was declared king. Henry never emerged from imprisonment and was murdered in the Tower shortly afterwards. It was an inglorious end to an unsuccessful reign.

Through succeeding generations, the Provost and Fellows of Eton were the manor's owners and involved in all aspects of its management. This included the responsibility for its tenants, incumbents and schoolmasters, the holding of regular courts and the granting of leases for enclosures, fields, houses, land, woods and a water mill. Eton's stewardship was to remain undisturbed for over 250 years until in 1799, at the outbreak of war, the government needed to both improve and increase the administration of its military supply lines and stores. Weedon Bec looked like a suitable location for a new centralised supplies organisation.

A proposal was made that the property could be joined to the Grand Union by the construction of a spur and in 1793 the work was put in hand. In 1799, Eton received compensation for the damage caused by the construction of the canal's embankments and footpaths and in 1801 the manor was put into trust, in advance of its sale. In 1803, an Act of Parliament was passed that confirmed its transfer to the government for industrial purposes and by 1804 plans to erect a barracks and factory had been agreed. Eton's long tenure was ended.

Appendix 2
Lieut. James King, RN, FRS, 1750-1784

James King was born in Clitheroe in 1750. His father was the rector at the time and later chaplain to the House of Commons and Dean of Raphoe in Ireland. James's parents had five sons of which James was the second. His brother, Walker, was a friend and executor to Edmund Burke and became Bishop of Rochester. A fourth son, Edward, brother of James, was the father of my great-great grandmother Dorothea who married Edward Hasell of Dalemain in Cumberland. Edward was vice-Chancellor of the Duchy of Lancaster and James's youngest brother, John, became Under-Secretary of the Treasury and Comptroller of army Accounts. They were a successful tribe.

James went to sea aged 12 from grammar school and entered the Royal Navy as a cadet midshipman under the patronage of his near relative, Captain Horton. The Seven Years war had ended and career prospects in the Service were restricted. James served under a number of commanders who had distinguished themselves including Rodney Palliser and St Vincent and was promoted to Lieutenant. However, James left the Royal Navy in 1774 because of his lack of prospects and went to Paris to learn French and improve his knowledge of science. His brother, Walker, was by then a member of Corpus Christi College, Oxford and arranged for James to join him there.

James's interest in, and proficiency at, mathematics attracted the attention of the university's professor of astronomy, Dr. Hornsby at the same time as the Admiralty under the Earl of Sandwich's leadership were considering commissioning an expedition to find the North West passage. Captain James Cook had already led two successful voyages of exploration and was invited to lead a third. A competent navigator was required and the Astronomer Royal, Maskelyne, was recommended by his Oxford colleague Hornsby to appoint James, a young man of undoubted talent.

On July 11th 1776, HMS *Resolution* in company with Cook's original vessel HMS *Discovery,* commanded by Captain Clerke, sailed from Plymouth. James was appointed second lieutenant and navigator to Cook on board the Resolution and in January 1777, the fleet reached Tasmania before sailing on to New Zealand. After sailing north again, following their instructions to find a North West passage, the expedition became entangled in pack ice and turned south towards the Sandwich Islands where they landed once more on Hawaii.

Meanwhile, James continued to develop his navigational skills by frequent observations in addition to his duties as lieutenant in watching keeping, trafficking with the islanders for provisions and supervising men sent ashore to find water.

After several weeks anchored in Karrakooa Bay, Cook took his leave planning to sail on to New Zealand again but a great storm blew up that wrecked the rigging of Resolution and he decided to set back to Hawaii for repairs. However, on arrival Cook and his crews found that all had changed. The local leaders were now hostile and a taboo had been placed on the bay and its landing grounds. Pilfering now became a serious and nightly nuisance and when Discovery's cutter was stolen, Cook determined on reprisals for its return. He organised a landing party for its recovery where it was met by stone throwing from a great crowd of locals. James had also landed to defend an observatory that had been set up on the shoreline to take measurements of the sun and stars and witnessed

> *"An immense crowd collected on the spot where Capt. Cook had just landed. We heard the firing of the musketry and could perceive some extraordinary bustle and agitation in the multitude. We afterwards saw the natives flying and I must confess that my heart soon misgave me."*

Cook's life was taken on July 2nd 1778 and the expedition, or what was left of it, sailed for home. James was first made lieutenant of the Resolution but on Clerke's death from consumption he returned to the Discovery and took command of the expedition. By September 1779 the little fleet had reached Macao and learned of the outbreak of the American War of Independence, reaching the Nore on 4th October 1780. James wrote the first and definitive account of the expedition and of Cook's death a year earlier.

The revolutionary war against America, France and Spain was now in progress and James was given command of HMS *Crocodile* and later a 40-gun frigate HMS *Resistance.* This was James's finest hour. He was appointed to command a large convoy of merchantmen to the West Indies which a French squadron out of Brest intended to intercept and destroy. As the convoy neared Jamaica, a fierce gale began to blow and it was believed that the French had got ahead and aimed to cut the convoy off before it reached its destination. James transferred his command to an armed cutter and, using his superior navigation skills, ordered the merchant ships to follow him through the darkness of the storm and enemy ships. Sailing behind James, those who followed his instructions reached the safety of Kingston harbour at daybreak. Not all the captains had obeyed his instructions and those who did not were taken by the French.

James returned to England in 1782 at the close of the war but his health had been ruined by his time at sea in foul conditions and his doctors proposed a healthier climate for his illness (consumption/TB). He was elected Fellow of the Royal Society in the same year for his contribution to science and exploration and moved to Nice where he died aged 34 in 1784. (After HEV)

Appendix 3
Acorn Flour & Bread

It was inevitable that the author should attempt to bake a loaf of bread using acorn flour. Purchased on Amazon UK, the outer packaging declared in Polish that the 500gm contents was the "traditional flour of our ancestors" and "full of fibre".

It is interesting to note that the flour came from a deeply rural area of Poland where oaks are widespread and where the local population still make bread from acorns as also happens in parts of Portugal and Spain.

Ingredients:

3 cups of warm water

2 tsp dried yeast

2 tsp honey

450 gm acorn flour

Directions:

Mix the flour, yeast, honey and water

Kneed the dough

Place in a bowl in a warm place (eg airing cupboard) for one hour

Kneed again and place in a bread pan for a further hour

Heat oven to 170° and bake for 35 minutes

The author was assisted throughout by his grand-daughter, Leila, who was the first to taste the result. She declared the bread disgusting and inedible!

Neanderthal bread

Archaeologists discovered that 70,000 years ago, a Neanderthal family living in a cave complex in Iraq cooked an assortment of wild grains, grasses and pulses that included lentils, pistachios and peas to make bread. The family smashed or ground the mixture before soaking it in water and baking it on a hot stone to produce a flatbread.

(from *The Times* newspaper 22/11/2022).

Ingredients:

Pulses

Dried peas

Fava beans

Lentils

Mustard seeds

Pistachio nuts

Directions

Soak for 24 hours. Grind and remove some of the husks (but not all). Mix in the mustard seeds and chopped pistachio nuts. Add water to form a thick paste. Bake on a hot stone.

Appendix 4
Oak gall ink

Oak galls were used to make ink throughout the Middle Ages. Galls are made when a gall wasp punctures the underside of an oak leaf and lays its egg. The oak leaf provides nutrition in the form of tannic and gallic acid and a round formation is created known as a gall nut or oak apple to protect the larvae. These 'nuts' can be harvested to make gall ink.

Ingredients

Oak galls

Water

Ferrous sulphate

Gum Arabic

Directions

Pulverise the oak galls by hand or in a kitchen mixer

Soak in 350 fl oz water and boil.

Filter through a cloth or coffee filter

Add 1fluid oz. of ferrous sulphate and leave for 24 hours.

(Ferrous sulphate can be made by soaking iron screws, etc. in water. Black tea can be used as an alternative)

Add ½ fluid oz. of gum Arabic, made from the Acacia tree (to thicken the ink and add brilliance)

Stir and dissolve

Bibliography

Abell W, *The Shipwright's Trade,* 1948, CUP

Adkins R, *Trafalgar, the biography of a battle,* 2004, ISBN 0-316-72551-0, Little, Brown London

Adkins R & Adkins L, *Jack Tar,* 2008, ISBN 978-1-4087-0054-9, Litle Brown, London

Albion R, *Forests & Sea Power,* 1926, Harvard University Press

Banbury P, *Shipbuilders of the Thames & Medway,* 1971, ISBN 0-7153-4996-1, David & Charles, Newton Abbot

Barnard J, *Building Britain's Wooden Walls,* 1997, ISBN 0-904614-63-8, Anthony Nelson, Oswestry

Basford K, *The Green Man,* 1978, ISBN 0-85991-497-6, DS Brewer, Woodbridge

Berg M, *The Age of Manufactures 1700-1820,* ISBN 1994, Routledge, London

Brindle S, *Brunel, The man who built the world,* 2005, ISBN 978-0-7538-2125-1, Weidenfeld & Nicholson, London

Bulley A, *The Bombay Country Ships,* 2000, ISBN 978-07007-123-66, Routledge, London

Captivating History, *The East India Company,* 2019, ASIN B083GK1FP6, Amazon UK, Kindle

Chatterton E, *The Old East Indiamen,* 1933, Rich & Cowan, London

Churchill WS, *A History of the English Speaking People, Vol 1, The birth of Britain,* 1956, Casell & Co, London

Clark J, *The Dissolution of the Monasteries,* 2021, ISBN 978-0-300-11572-7, Yale University Press, New Haven

Clayton T & Craig P, *Trafalgar, the men, the battle, the storm,* 2004, CN 132133, BCA, London

Colville Q & Davey J, *Nelson Navy & Nation,* 2013, ISBN 97818-448-62078, Anova Books, London

Dalrymple W, *The Anarchy, 2019,* ASIN B07VPR8L51, Bloomsbury, London

Darwin J, *Unfinished Empire,* 2013, ISBN 978-18461408-9-1, Penguin, London

Davies JD, *Pepys's Navy,* 2008, 978-4738-7928-7, Seaforth, Pen & Sword, Barnsley

Davis R, *The rise of the English Shipping Industry,* 1962, ISBN 0-7153-54621-0, David & Charles, Newton Abbot

Ennos R, *The Wood Age,* 2021, ISBN 978-0-00-831883-3, William Collins, London

Fass M, *Napoleon@bay,* 2021, ISBN 978-1-913663-89-6, Biddles Books, King's Lynn

——, *The Royal Berkshire Regiment, The early Years, 1758-1815,*

2021, ISBN 978-1-913663-75-9, Biddles Books, King's Lynn

Feather M, *HMS Amphion 1798,* 1998, ISBN 09536-169-08, Feather, Suffolk

Fletcher R, *In the days of the Tall Ships,* 2008, ISBN 978-144373745-3, Home Farm Books, Worcester

Grant J, *The War of the Austrian Succession,* 2018, ISBN 178282715-3, Leonaur, London

Hannay D, *Ships and Men,* ASIN VB001BVMM, 1910, Blackwood, Edinburgh

Harris E, Harris J & James N, *Oak, A British History,* 2003, ISBN 0-9538630-8-5, Windgatherer Press Macclesfield

Hayward P, *Surgeon Henry's Trifles,* 1970, ISBN 7011-1569-6, Chatto & Windus, London

Jeffs A, *Storyland, a new mythology of Britain,* 202, ISBN 978-1-529407-976, Riverrun, London

Johnson L, *Shadow King,* 1988, ISBN 978-1784-979-645, head of Zeus, London

Keay J, *The Honourable Company,* 1993, ISBN 0-00-638072-7, Harper Collins, London

Knight R, Britain against Napoleon, 2013, ISBN 978-0-141-03894-0, Penguin, London

Knighton C, *Pepys and the Navy,* 2003, ISBN 0-7509-2972-3, Sutton Publishing, Stroud

Konstam A, *Mutiny on the Spanish Main,* 2020. ASIN B877CVJ72, Osprey, Oxford

——, *Tudor Warships (1),* 2008, ISBN 978-1-84603-251-6, Osprey, London

——, *Tudor Warships (2),* 2008, ISBN 978-1-84603- 252-3, Osprey, London

Langford S, *Rooted,* 2022, ISBN 978-0-241-10374-4, Penguin, London

Lavery B, *Life in Nelson's Navy,* 2007, ISBN 978-0-7509-4774-3, Sutton Publishing, London

——, *Empire of the Seas,* 2009, ISBN 07818-4486-1095, Anova Books, London

——, *Nelson's Navy, The ships, men and organisation,* 1989, ISBN 0-85177-521-7, Conway Maritime Press, London

Lewis J, *From gunpowder to guns,* 2009, ISBN 978-1904-750857, RSA Trust, Middlesex University, London

Lewis-Sempel J, *The glorious life of the Oak,* 2018, ISBAN 978-08575-581-9, Penguin, London

Logan W, *Oak, the frame of civilisation,* 2005, ISBN 13-978-0-393-32778-6, Norton, New York

Macdougall P, *The Chatham Dockyard story,* 1981, ISBN 0848193-301, Meresborough Books, Rainham, Kent

——, *Royal Dockyards,* 1989, ISBN 0-7478-0033-2, Shire Publications, Aylesbury

Maclean A, *Captain Cook,* 1972, ISBN 0-00-211143-8, Collins, london

Masefield J, *Sea Life in Nelson's time,* 1972, Sphere Books, London

Matthews R, *The Spanish Armada,* 2009, ISBN 978-0-7524-5363-1, Spellmount, Stroud

McDougall D, *The Country Blacksmith,* 2013, ISBN 13-978-074781-231-9, Shire Library, Bloomsbury, Oxford

McLynn F, *1759, The year Britain became master of the world,* 2004, ISBN 0-224-06245-x, Random House, London

Miles A, *The British Oak,* 2013, ISBN 978-1-47212-375-6, Little, Brown, London

Moorhouse G, *Great Harry's Navy,* 2006, ISBN 13-978-0-7538-2099-5, Weidenfeld & Nicholson, London

Morgan M, *The English Lads of the Abbey of Bec,* 1946, OUP, London

Morris M, The *Anglo Saxons,* 2021, ISBN 978-1786-330-994, Penguin, London

Nancollas T, *The Ship Asunder,* 2022, ISBN 978-0-241-43414-7, Penguin, London

Nester W, *Britain's rise to global superpower in the age of Napoleon,* 2020, ISBN 978-152677543-6, Frontline Books,

Peal R, *Meet the Georgians,* 2021, ISBN 978-0-00-843702-2, William Collins, London

Presnail J, *Chatham,* 1952, The Corporation of Chatham

Pocock T, *Captain Marryat,* 2000, ISBN 1-86176-130-9, Duckworth & Co, London

——, *Battle for Empire,* 1998, ISBN 1-85479-332-2, O'Mara Books, London

Pole A, *Blacksmith: Apprentice to Master,* 2021, ISBN 978-1787-713-6458, Quadrille Publishing, Amazon UK (Kindle)

Regan G, *Naval Blunders,* 2001, ISBN 0-233-99978-7, Andre Deutsch, London

Rodger N, *The Wooden World,* 1988, ISBN 0-00-686152-0, Fontana, London

Simard S, *Finding the Mother Tree,* 2021, ISBN 978-0-141-99028-6, Penguin Books, London

Summers WH, *The Lollards of the Chiltern Hills,* 1906, ISBN 979-867-607-162, Francis Griffiths, London

Sutton J, *Lords of the East,* 1981. ISBN 0-85177-169-6, Conway Maritime Press, London

Tallamy DW, *The Nature of Oaks*, 2021, ISBN 978-1-64326-044-0, Timber Press, Portland

Tree I, *Wilding,* 2018, ISBN 978-1-5098-0509-9, Macmillan, London

Tute W, *The True Glory,* 1983, ISBN 0-356-10403-6, Macdonald & Co., London

Uglow J, *In These Times,* 2014, ISBN 978-0-571-26952-5, Faber & Faber, London

Wilkinson-Latham R, *The Royal Navy, 1790-1970,* 1977, ISBN 0-85045-248-1, Osprey, London

Wilson B, *Empire of the Deep,* 2013, ISBN 978-0-7538-2920-2, Orion Books, London

Winfield R, *British warships in the age of sail,* 2007, ASIN BookSB72GO, Seaforth Publishing on Amazon UK (Kindle)